BLAND FANATICS

BLAND FANATICS

LIBERALS,

RACE,

AND EMPIRE

PANKAJ MISHRA

FARRAR, STRAUS AND GIROUX | NEW YORK

Farrar, Straus and Giroux
120 Broadway, New York 10271

Printed in the United States of America
Originally published in 2020 by Verso, Great Britain
Published in the United States by Farrar, Straus and Giroux
First American edition, 2020

These essays previously appeared, in slightly different form, in the
following publications: *The Guardian* (chapters 2, 3, 4, and 6),
the *London Review of Books* (chapters 1, 5, 6, 7, 10, 11, 12, and 13),
The New York Times (chapters 8 and 14), *The New York Review of
Books* (chapter 9), and *The New Yorker* (chapter 15).

Library of Congress Control Number: 2020939306
ISBN: 978-0-374-29331-4

Our books may be purchased in bulk for promotional, educational,
or business use. Please contact your local bookseller or the Macmillan
Corporate and Premium Sales Department at 1-800-221-7945, extension
5442, or by e-mail at MacmillanSpecialMarkets@macmillan.com.

www.fsgbooks.com
www.twitter.com/fsgbooks • www.facebook.com/fsgbooks

1   3   5   7   9   10   8   6   4   2

Contents

Introduction

I Want Everyone to Become an American

Thomas Friedman

*Someday we must write the history of our own obscurity –
manifest the density of our narcissism*

Roland Barthes

The essays in this book were written in response to the Anglo-American delusions that climaxed in Brexit, the election of Donald Trump and, finally, a calamitous response to the COVID-19 outbreak. These range from the nineteenth-century dream of imperial-era liberalism long championed by the *Economist*, in which capital, goods, jobs and people freely circulate, through Henry Luce's proclamation of an 'American century' of free trade and 'modernisation theory' – the attempt by American Cold Warriors to seduce the post-colonial world away from communist-style revolution and into the gradualist alternative of consumer capitalism and democracy – to the catastrophic humanitarian wars and demagogic explosions of our times.

'Among the lesser culprits of history', Reinhold Niebuhr wrote in 1957, at the height of the Cold War, 'are the bland fanatics of western civilization who regard the highly contingent achievements of our culture as the final form and norm of human existence.' For Niebuhr, the bigger culprits of history were, of course, communists and fascists. A dedicated anti-communist, the American theologian was vulnerable to phrases such as 'the moral superiority of Western civilization'. Nevertheless, he could see the peculiar trajectory of liberalism: how 'a dogma which was intended to guarantee the economic freedom of the individual became the "ideology" of vast corporate structures of a later period of capitalism, used by them, and still used, to prevent a proper political control of their power'. He was also alert to the fundamentalist creed that has shaped our age – that Western-style capitalism and liberal democracy will be gradually generalised around the world, and every society, in short, ought to evolve just as Britain and the United States did.

Of course, Niebuhr could not have anticipated that the bland fanatics who made the Cold War so treacherous would come to occupy, at its end, history's centre stage. Incarnated as liberal internationalists, neocon democracy promoters and free-market globalisers, they would blunder through a world grown more complex and intractable, and help unravel large parts of Asia, Africa and Latin America before sowing political chaos in their own societies.

The global history of the post-1945 ideologies of liberalism and democracy, or a comprehensive sociology of Anglo-America and Anglo- and America-philic intellectuals, is yet to be written, though the world they made and unmade is entering its most treacherous phase yet. Most of us are still only emerging, bleary-eyed, from the frenetic post–Cold War decades when, as Don DeLillo wrote, 'the dramatic climb of the Dow and the speed of the internet summoned us all to live permanently in the future, in the utopian glow of cyber-capital'.

But it has long been clear that the global wager on unregulated markets, and military interventions on behalf of them, were the most ambitious ideological experiments undertaken in the modern era. Their adepts, allies and facilitators, from Greece to Indonesia, were also far more influential than their socialist and communist rivals. *Homo economicus*, the autonomous, reasoning, rights-bearing subject of liberal philosophy, came to stalk all societies with some fantastical plans to universally escalate production and consumption. The vernacular of modernity coined in London, New York and Washington, DC, came to define the common sense of public intellectual life across all continents, radically altering the way in which much of the world's population understood society, economy, nation, time and individual and collective identity.

Of course, those trying to look beyond the exalted rhetoric of liberal politics and economics rarely found any corresponding realities. My own education in this absence began through an experience of Kashmir, where India, billed as the world's largest democracy, descended into a form of Hindu supremacism and racist imperialism of the kind it liberated itself from in 1947. I went to the valley in 1999 with many of the prejudices of the liberal Indian 'civiliser' – someone who placidly assumed that Kashmiri Muslims were much better off being aligned with 'secular', 'liberal' and 'democratic' India than with the Islamic state of Pakistan.

The brutal realities of India's military occupation of Kashmir and the blatant falsehoods and deceptions that accompanied it forced me to revisit many of the old critiques of Western imperialism and its rhetoric of progress. When my critical articles on Kashmir appeared in the year 2000 in the *Hindu* and the *New York Review of Books*, they were attacked at home most vociferously by self-styled custodians of India's 'liberal democracy' rather than by Hindu nationalists. I had come up against an influential ideology of Indian exceptionalism, which claimed moral prestige and geopolitical significance for India's uniquely massive and diverse liberal democracy.

Many of those righteous notions reeked of upper-caste sanctimony and class privilege. Piously invoking the 'idea of India', the country's experiment with a secular and liberal polity, the fetishists of formal and procedural democracy seemed unbothered by the fact that people in Kashmir and India's north-eastern border states lived under de facto martial law, where security forces had unlimited licence to massacre and rape, or that a great majority of the Indian population found the promise of equality and dignity underpinned by rule of law and impartial institutions to be a remote, almost fantastical, ideal.

For decades, India benefited from a Cold War-era conception of 'democracy', which reduced it to a morally glamorous label for the way rulers are elected, rather than for the kinds of power they hold, or the ways they exercise it. As a non-communist country that held routine elections, India possessed a matchless international prestige despite consistently failing – worse than many Asian, African and Latin American countries – to provide its citizens with even the basic components of a dignified existence. The halo of virtue around India shone brighter as its governments embraced free markets and communist-run China abruptly emerged as a challenger to the West. Even as India descended into Hindu nationalism, an exuberant consensus about India was developing among Anglo-American elites: that liberal democracy had acquired deep roots in Indian soil, fertilising it for the growth of free markets.

For a writer of my background, it became imperative to challenge this unanimity – first at home, and then, increasingly, abroad. In many ways, India's own bland fanatics, who seemed determined to nail their cherished 'idea of India' into Kashmiri hearts and minds, prepared me for the spectacle of a liberal intelligentsia cheerleading the war for 'human rights' in Iraq, with the kind of humanitarian rhetoric about freedom, democracy and progress that was originally heard from European imperialists in the nineteenth century.

It had long been clear to me that Western ideologues during the Cold War absurdly prettified the rise of the 'democratic' West. The long struggle against communism, which claimed superior moral virtue, had required many expedient feints. The centuries of civil war, imperial conquest, brutal exploitation and genocide were suppressed in accounts that showed how Westerners made the modern world, and became with their liberal democracies the superior people everyone else ought to catch up with. What I didn't realise until I started to inhabit the knowledge ecosystems of London and New York is how evasions and suppressions had resulted, over time, in a massive store of defective knowledge about the West and the non-West alike. Simple-minded and misleading ideas and assumptions, drawn from this blinkered history, had come to shape the speeches of Western statesmen, think tank reports and newspaper editorials, while supplying fuel to countless log-rolling columnists, television pundits and terrorism experts.

It may be hard to remember today, especially for younger readers, that the mainstream of Anglo-America in the early 2000s deferentially hosted figures like Niall Ferguson, and arguments that the occupation and subjugation of other people's territory and culture were an efficacious instrument of civilisation, and that we needed more such emancipatory imperialism to bring intransigently backward peoples in line with the advanced West. Astonishingly, British imperialism, seen for decades by Western scholars and anti-colonial leaders alike as a racist, illegitimate and often predatory despotism, came to be repackaged in our own time as a benediction that, in Ferguson's words, 'undeniably pioneered free trade, free capital movements and, with the abolition of slavery, free labour'.

Never mind that free trade, introduced to Asia through gunboats, destroyed nascent industry in conquered countries, that 'free' capital mostly went to the white settler states of Australia and Canada, and that indentured rather than 'free' labour replaced slavery. The fairy tales about how Britain made the modern world weren't just aired at some furtive far-right conclave or hedge funders' luxury retreat. Mainstream television, radio, and the broadsheets took the lead in making them seem intellectually respectable to a wide audience. Politicians as well as broadcasters deferred to their belligerent illogic. The BBC set aside prime time for Niall Ferguson's belief in the necessity of reinstating imperialism. The Tory minister for education asked him to advise on the history syllabus. Looking for a more authoritative audience, the revanchists then crossed the Atlantic to provide an intellectual armature to Americans trying to remake the modern world through free markets and military force.

Of course, the bards of a new universal liberal empire almost entirely suppressed Asian, African and Latin American voices. And the very few allowed access to the mainstream press found that their unique privilege obliged them to, first of all, clear the ground of misrepresentations and downright falsehoods that had built up over decades. This often frustrating struggle defined my own endeavour, reflected in the pages that follow.

It was hard to avoid, for the prejudices were deeply entrenched in every realm of journalistic endeavour, looming up obdurately whether one wrote about Afghanistan, India or Japan. To give one example: In *Free to Choose*, a hugely influential book (and ten-part television series), Milton and Rose Friedman had posed a seductive binary of rational markets versus inter-fering governments (what came to underpin World Bank and International Monetary Fund reports, policies and prescrip-tions for the next two decades). Friedman, who inspired the 'Chicago Boys' re-engineering Chile's economy after the CIA ousted Salvador Allende in 1973, sought intellectual vindication in East Asia, claiming that Japan, South Korea, Taiwan, Hong Kong and Singapore had succeeded owing to their reliance on 'private markets'. In *The End of History and the Last Man*, Francis Fukuyama echoed this assertion, arguing that East Asia's economies, by 'repeating the experience of Germany and Japan in the late nineteenth and early twentieth centuries, have proven that economic liberalism allows late modernizers to catch up with and even overtake' the West.

This fable about the East Asian 'miracle', then, became central to mainstream reporting about Asia. It did not tally at all with the historical record, which showed that state-led modernisation

and economic protectionism were as central to the economies of pre-war Japan and Germany as to post-war East Asia;
more recently, the long traditions of technocratic governance
in East Asia have proven crucial to its relatively successful
response to the coronavirus pandemic while Anglo-American
free-marketeers lethally flounder. But such facts about 'state
intervention', as blithely ignored in the *New York Times* as in
the *Economist* and the *Wall Street Journal*, seemed to engage
very few people.

Of course, the fables about free markets just happened to
match the efforts of the World Bank, the IMF and other institutions of international economic management, whose priorities
of poverty alleviation and public sector development had given
way by the early 1980s to privatisation, trade deregulation, the
reduction of price subsidies and relaxation of limits on foreign
investments. By the time the Soviet Union imploded and an
army of Americanisers invaded Russia, the free-marketeers
were emboldened enough to think they had the power, as in
Reagan's favourite line from Thomas Paine, 'to begin the world
over again'. Saul Bellow, writing to a friend in 1992, warned
that 'the free-market economic theorists have done too well.
They have taught the country that laissez faire won the cold
war'. The aggressive promotion of a new form of what Albert
Hirschman called 'mono-economics' was accompanied by the
breathtaking conceit that the fall of communism had inaugurated a benignly post-ideological age. As it turned out, those
hoping to begin the world over again by administering economic
shock therapy to Russia were not disappointed. Living standards
collapsed; Russia suffered a severe mortality crisis, resulting in
millions of additional male deaths in the 1990s; and the crime
rate skyrocketed – a series of disasters that culminated in the
destruction of the rouble and bankruptcy in 1998.

Having planted their flag over the Kremlin, the crusaders were
eyeing new conquests around the world. By the late 1990s, there
were many powerful and wealthy sponsors of the Washington

consensus that was being imposed on Latin America, Asia and Africa. New centres of intellectual and political authority had emerged in American universities, business schools and philanthropic foundations. Non-Americans rose to senior positions in American-dominated international institutions such as the World Bank and the IMF. Today, right-wing think tanks such as the American Enterprise Institute, the Cato Institute and the Peterson Institute employ many more economists and journalists of non-American origin.

Much of the work of exporting the iron cages of American modernity was increasingly done, by the early 2000s, by foreign-born academics and think-tankers, who interfaced resourcefully between the elites of their ancestral and adopted countries. A prominent example of such intellectual synergy is Jagdish Bhagwati, in his own words the 'world's foremost free-trader' and the godfather of India's marketised economy. From his pulpit at Columbia University and the Council for Foreign Relations, Bhagwati and his disciples kept up a drumbeat of neo-liberal ideas arguing that no nation can advance without reining in labour unions, eliminating trade barriers, ending subsidies, etc.

Even the terrorist attacks of 9/11 did not shake such convictions. The suspicion that 'Islamo-fascism' had declared war on liberalism actually roused many Anglo-American intellectuals into a bolder attempt to make the world over again in their preferred image of Anglo-America. Modernisation theorists, respectful of the *longue durée* in history, had entrusted the nurturing of democracy to middle-class beneficiaries of capitalism. But a 'post-ideological' generation of liberal internationalists as well as neocons now thought that democracy could be implanted through shock-and-awe therapy in societies that had no tradition of it.

In their dominant discourse, the racial and religious 'other' was either an irredeemable brute, the exact opposite of rationally self-interested Americans, to be exterminated universally through a relentless war on terror, or an American-style *homo economicus* who was prevented from pursuing his rational self-interest by his deficient political leaders and institutions. In the fantasy that drove the invasion and occupation of Iraq, freedom miraculously appears when the despotic state is emasculated and free markets, finally allowed to flourish, spontaneously harmonise individual interests and desires.

More importantly, the terrorist attacks on September 11 provoked an assertion of civilisational identity and solidarity, paving the way for more overt expressions of white supremacism. A small group of criminals and fanatics did not pose a mortal threat to the most powerful and wealthy societies in history. Nevertheless, the maniacal cries of 'Allahu Akbar' were met by a louder drumbeat of 'Western values' and confidence-building invocations of the West's apparent quintessence, such as the Enlightenment. The collective affirmations of certain Western freedoms and privileges – 'we must agree on what matters: kissing in public places, bacon sandwiches, disagreement, cutting-edge fashion', Salman Rushdie wrote – became an emotional reflex. Susan Sontag seemed tactless to many in speaking of the 'sanctimonious, reality-concealing rhetoric' of 'confidence-building and grief management' that resembled the 'unanimously applauded, self-congratulatory bromides of a Soviet Party Congress'. She was attacked for insisting, 'Let's by all means grieve together, but let's not be stupid together.'

Her warnings went unheeded. 'I'm happy to be a laptop general,' Paul Berman wrote in *Terror and Liberalism*, reprimanding those unwilling to join the new crusade for liberalism in the Middle East. During the Vietnam War, Hannah Arendt noted that members of the Democratic Administration had frequent recourse to phrases like 'monolithic communism' and 'second Munich' and deduced from this an inability 'to confront reality on its own terms because they had always some parallels in mind that "helped" them to understand those terms'. Similarly,

Berman, who wasn't known previously for his expertise on modern political movements east of Europe, identified Islamism as a derivative version of the totalitarian enemies – fascism and communism – that liberalism had already fought throughout the twentieth century. After 'trolling the Islamic bookstores of Brooklyn', he offered a genealogy of 'Islamism' that rested almost entirely on his reading of Sayyid Qutb, an ideologue of the Egyptian Muslim Brotherhood. According to Berman, liberal intellectuals were obliged to do battle with the new nihilistic fascism, which included secular dictatorships like Iraq's as well as pan-Islamist movements. His laptop bombing quickly united a variety of public figures, from Richard Holbrooke to Martin Amis, in the cause.

Martin Amis published an essay on Islam and Islamism, which went on for more than 10,000 words without describing an individual experience of Muslim societies deeper than Christopher Hitchens's acquisition of an Osama T-shirt in Peshawar and the Amis family's failure to enter, after closing time, the Dome of the Rock in Jerusalem. 'The impulse towards rational inquiry', Amis asserted, 'is by now very weak in the rank and file of the Muslim male.' There were countless other startling claims (according to Amis, the army was on the Islamist side in the Algerian civil war) in his essay, whose pseudo-scholarship and fanatical conviction of moral superiority made it resemble nothing more than one of bin Laden's desperately literary screeds.

Among the literati, big words like 'Salafist totalitarianism' and 'Islamo-fascism' helped project the illusion of profound knowledge. They also satisfied the nostalgic desire of some sedentary writers to see themselves in the avant-garde of a noble crusade against an evil '-ism'. The fervour of the ideologue *manqué* made no room for the sober fact that almost every nation state harbours a disaffected and volatile minority, whose size varies constantly in inverse relation to the alertness, tact and wisdom of the majority population.

It was a demoralising spectacle: talented writers nibbling on clichés picked to the bone by tabloid hacks, and a counterfeit imperial history and minatory visions of frenziedly breeding Muslims being enlisted in large-scale violence against voiceless peoples. But, as Niebuhr pointed out, the 'men of culture', with their developed faculty of reasoning, tend to 'give the hysterias of war and the imbecilities of national politics more plausible excuses than the average man is capable of inventing'. As it happened, the 'public conversation' about Islam proposed by Amis was never held. Its terms had been set too low, and it came to be dominated by an isolated and vain chattering class that, all shook up by a changing world, sought to reassure themselves and us by digging an unbridgeable Maginot Line around our minds and hearts.

Meanwhile, neo-imperialist assaults on Iraq and Afghanistan served to highlight the actual legacy of British imperialism: tribal, ethnic and religious conflicts that stifled new nation states at birth or doomed them to endless civil war punctuated by ruthless despotisms. Defeat and humiliation were compounded by the revelation that those charged with bringing civilisation from the West to the rest indulged – yet again – in indiscriminate murder and torture.

Ardent young socio-economic engineers imported from America to Baghdad's Green Zone tried to achieve everything in Iraq that the free-marketeers hoped for at home – the abolition of welfare, privatisation of the military and prisons, and general deregulation. This most audacious experiment yet in Americanisation not only provoked a ferocious insurgency; it triggered the break-up of the country, the rise of Islamic State and the unravelling of the Middle East. Chaos and mass suffering in Russia had already helped to turn a dour former KGB operative, Vladimir Putin, into his country's unlikely saviour (and brazen meddler in America's own elections).

Eventually, the disappointed and disaffected in the very heartland of liberal modernity turned a serial groper into their saviour. As Donald Trump's victory in November 2016 revealed, the Washington consensus had created too many victims in Washington, DC's own hinterland. While the battle for democracy and capitalism raged in the Levant, they were being steadily undermined west of the Potomac by extreme concentrations of wealth, the steady criminalisation of the poor, dysfunctional politics, a rogue security establishment and a heedless media.

More than a decade after September 11, the reality-concealing rhetoric of Western liberalism kept participating in a race to extremes with its ideological twin, in an escalated dialectic of bombing from the air and slaughter on the ground. It grew more aggressive in proportion to the spread of the non-West's chaos to the West, and also blended faster into a white supremacist hatred of immigrants, refugees and Muslims (and, often, those who just 'look' Muslim). Even more menacingly, it postponed the moment of self-reckoning and course correction among Anglo-American elites.

In one of his last interviews, Tony Judt lamented his 'catastrophic' Anglo-American generation whose cossetted members included George W. Bush and Tony Blair. Having grown up after the defining wars and hatreds of the West's twentieth century, 'in a world of no hard choices, neither economic nor political', these historically weightless elites believed that 'no matter what choice they made, there would be no disastrous consequences.' A member of the Bush administration brashly affirmed its arrogance of power in 2004 after what then seemed a successful invasion of Iraq: 'When we act,' he boasted, 'we create our own reality.'

'A pretty crappy generation,' Judt concluded, 'when you come to think of it.' In the end, its retro megalomania could not be sustained in a world where, for better and for worse, cultural as well as economic power was leaking away from the old Anglo-American establishment. An enlarged global public society, with its many dissenting and corrective voices, emerged in the last decade; today, it quickly calls the bluff of lavishly credentialled intellectual elites.

A great correction is under way today, with triumphalist narratives of British and American exceptionalism interrogated as stringently as the post-colonial claims to virtue once were. The coronavirus cruelly exposed the reality they had long concealed: heavily indebted states, bailed-out corporations, impoverished working classes, and eviscerated public health systems. Anglo-American self-deceptions, which always exacted a high death toll abroad, from the Irish famine to Iraq, have become mass-murderous at home; a blusteringly casual attitude to the pandemic has resulted in tens of thousands of premature deaths in Britain and the United States. The world as we have known it, moulded by the beneficiaries of both Western imperialism and anti-imperialist nationalism, is crumbling. Many of our exalted ideas about ourselves have collapsed. India's claims to exceptionalism appear to have been as unfounded as America's own. Fresh and broader struggles for freedom, equality and dignity loom. But, as the later essays in this collection point out, the newly emergent voices in the public sphere are still likely to be drowned out by loud and repetitive lamentations about the loss of Anglo-American poise and virtue.

These became especially loud after Boris Johnson joined Donald Trump in the leadership of the free world. From the Cold War through to the 'war on terror', the Caesarism that afflicted other nations was seen as peculiar to Asian and African peoples or blamed on the despotic traditions of Russians or Chinese, on African tribalism, Islam or the 'Arab mind'. But this analysis – amplified in a thousand books and opinion columns that located the enemies of democracy among menacingly alien people and their inferior cultures – did not prepare its audience for the sight of blond bullies and bunglers perched atop the world's greatest democracies. The barbarians, it turns out, were never at the gate; they have been ruling us for some time.

The belated shock of this realisation has made impotent

despair the dominant tone of establishment commentary on the events of the past few years. But this acute helplessness betrays something more significant. While democracy was being hollowed out in the West, mainstream politicians and columnists concealed its growing void by thumping their chests against its supposed foreign enemies – or cheerleading its supposed foreign friends. Decades of this deceptive and deeply ideological discourse have left many of our best and brightest stultified by the antics of Trump and Johnson, simultaneously aghast at the sharpened critiques of a resurgent left, and profoundly unable to reckon with the annihilation of democracy by its supposed friends abroad.

The vulnerabilities of Western democracy were evident long ago to the Asian and African subjects of the British Empire. Gandhi, who saw democracy as literally the rule of the people, the *demos*, claimed that it was merely 'nominal' in the West. It could have no reality so long as 'the wide gulf between the rich and the hungry millions persists' and voters 'take their cue from their newspapers, which are often dishonest'. Inaugurating India's own experiment with an English-style parliament and electoral system, B. R. Ambedkar, one of the main authors of the Indian constitution, warned that while the principle of one person, one vote conferred political equality, it left untouched grotesque social and economic inequalities. 'We must remove this contradiction at the earliest possible moment,' he urged, 'or else those who suffer from inequality will blow up the structure of political democracy.' Today's elected demagogues, who were chosen by aggrieved voters precisely for their skills in blowing up political democracy, have belatedly alerted many more to this contradiction. But the delay in heeding Ambedkar's warning has been lethal.

What has become clearer since the coronavirus crisis is that modern democracies have for decades been lurching towards moral and ideological bankruptcy – unprepared by their own publicists to cope with the political and environmental disasters that unregulated capitalism ceaselessly inflicts, even on such winners of history as Britain and the US. Having laboured to exclude a smelly past of ethnocide, slavery and racism – and the ongoing stink of corporate venality – from their perfumed notion of Anglo-American superiority, the bland fanatics have no nose for democracy's true enemies.

Besieged both at home and abroad, their authority as over-lords, policemen and interpreters of the globe is increasingly challenged. If they repetitively ventilate their rage and frustration, or whinge incessantly about 'cancel culture' and the 'radical left', it is because that is all they can do. Their own mind-numbing simplicities about democracy, its enemies, friends, the free world and all that sort of thing, have doomed them to experience the contemporary world as an endless series of shocks and debacles. If rage, confusion and bewilderment mark their visages, it is because, today, their narcissism lies shattered, self-congratulation can no longer pose as an analytical framework, and rancorous ethno-nationalism in India and criminally inept autocrats in Britain and America have bluntly clarified that liberal democracy is not what we have – at least, not yet.

1

Watch This Man

On Niall Ferguson and Neo-imperialism

'Civilisation's going to pieces,' Tom Buchanan, the Yale-educated millionaire, abruptly informs Nick Carraway in *The Great Gatsby*. 'I've gotten to be a terrible pessimist about things. Have you read *The Rise of the Colored Empires* by this man Goddard? . . . The idea is if we don't look out the white race will be – will be utterly submerged.' 'Tom's getting very profound,' his wife Daisy remarks. Buchanan carries on: 'This fellow has worked out the whole thing. It's up to us, who are the dominant race, to watch out or these other races will have control of things.' 'We've got to beat them down,' Daisy whispers with a wink at Nick. But there's no stopping Buchanan. 'And we've produced all the things that go to make civilisation – oh, science and art, and all that. Do you see?'

'There was something pathetic in his concentration,' Carraway, the narrator, observes, 'as if his complacency, more acute than of old, was not enough to him any more.' The scene, early in the novel, helps identify Buchanan as a bore – and a boor. It also evokes a deepening panic among America's Anglophile ruling class. Wary of Jay Gatz, the self-made man with a fake Oxbridge pedigree, Buchanan is nervous about other upstarts rising out of nowhere to challenge the master race.

Scott Fitzgerald based Goddard, at least partly, on Theodore Lothrop Stoddard, the author of the bestseller *The Rising Tide of Color against White World-Supremacy*. Stoddard's fame was a sign of his times, of the overheated racial climate of the early twentieth century, in which the Yellow Peril seemed real, the Ku Klux Klan had re-emerged, and Theodore Roosevelt worried loudly about 'race-suicide'. In 1917, justifying his reluctance to involve the United States in the European war, Woodrow Wilson told his secretary of state that 'white civilisation and its domination over the world rested largely on our ability to keep this country intact'.

Hysteria about 'white civilisation' gripped America after Europe's self-mutilation in the First World War had encouraged political assertiveness among subjugated peoples from Egypt to China. Unlike other popular racists, who parsed the differences between Nordic and Latin peoples, Stoddard proposed a straightforward division of the world into white and coloured races. He also invested early in Islamophobia, arguing in *The New World of Islam* that Muslims posed a sinister threat to a hopelessly fractious and confused West. Like many respectable eugenicists of his time, Stoddard later found much to like about the Nazis, which marked him out for instant superannuation following the exposure of Nazi crimes in 1945.

The banner of white supremacism has been more warily raised ever since in post-imperial Europe, and very rarely by mainstream politicians and writers. In the United States, racial anxieties have been couched either in such pseudo-scientific tracts about the inferiority of certain races as *The Bell Curve*, or in big alarmist theories like Samuel Huntington's 'clash of civilisations'. It's not at all surprising that in his last book Huntington fretted about the destruction by Latino immigration of America's national identity, which is apparently a construct of 'Anglo-Protestant culture'. As power ostensibly shifts to the East, a counterpoise to dismay over the West's loss of authority and influence is sought in a periodic ballyhooing of the 'transatlantic alliance', as in Philip Bobbitt's *Terror and Consent*, which Niall Ferguson in an enthusiastic review claimed will 'be read with pleasure by men of a certain age, class and education from Manhattan's Upper East Side to London's West End'.

Ferguson himself is *homo atlanticus* redux. In a preface to the UK edition of *Civilisation: The West and the Rest*, he writes of being seduced away from a stodgy Oxbridge career, early in the 2000s, to the United States, 'where the money and power actually were'. The author of two previous books about nineteenth-century banking, Ferguson became known to the general public with *The Pity of War*, a long polemic, fluent and bristling with scholarly references, that blamed Britain for causing the First World War. According to Ferguson, Prussia wasn't the threat it was made out to be by Britain's Liberal Cabinet. The miscalculation not only made another war inevitable after 1919, and postponed the creation of an inevitably German-dominated European Union to the closing decades of the twentieth century; it also tragically and fatally weakened Britain's grasp on its overseas possessions.

This wistful vision of an empire on which the sun need never have set had an immediately obvious defect. It grossly underestimated – in fact, ignored altogether – the growing strength of anti-colonial movements across Asia, which, whatever happened in Europe, would have undermined Britain's dwindling capacity to manage its vast overseas holdings. At the time, however, *The Pity of War* seemed boyishly and engagingly revisionist, and it established Ferguson's reputation: he was opinionated, 'provocative' and amusing, all things that seem to be more cherished in Britain's intellectual culture than in any other.

In retrospect, *The Pity of War*'s Stoddardesque laments about the needless emasculation of Anglo-Saxon power announced a theme that would become more pronounced as Ferguson, setting aside his expertise in economic history, emerged as an evangelist-cum-historian of empire. He was already arguing in *The Cash Nexus*, published a few months before the terrorist attacks of 11 September 2001, that 'the United States should be devoting a larger percentage of its vast resources to making the world safe for capitalism and democracy' – if necessary by military force. 'Let me come clean,' he wrote in the *New York Times Magazine* in April 2003, a few weeks after the shock-and-awe campaign began in Iraq, 'I am a fully paid-up member of the neoimperialist gang.'

Empire: How Britain Made the Modern World, Ferguson's next book, appeared in America with a more didactic subtitle: 'The Rise and Demise of the British World Order and the Lessons for Global Power'. The word 'empire' still caused some unease in the US, whose own national myths originated in an early, short-lived and selective anti-imperialism. An exasperated Ferguson – 'the United States', he claimed, 'is an empire, in short, that dare not speak its name' – set out to rescue the word from the discredit into which political correctness had apparently cast it. Britain's nineteenth-century empire 'undeniably pioneered free trade, free capital movements and, with the abolition of slavery, free labour. It invested immense sums in developing a global network of modern communications. It spread and enforced the rule of law over vast areas.' 'Without the spread of British rule around the world', he went on, in a typical counterfactual manoeuvre, colonised peoples, such as Indians, would not have what are now their most valuable ideas and institutions – parliamentary democracy, individual freedom and the English language.

America should now follow Britain's example, Ferguson argued, neglecting to ask why it needed to make the modern world if Britain had already done such a great job. He agreed with the neocon Max Boot that the United States should re-create across Asia the 'enlightened foreign administration once provided by self-confident Englishmen in jodhpurs and pith helmets'. 'The work needs to begin, and swiftly,' he wrote, 'to encourage American students at the country's leading universities to think more seriously about careers overseas.'

Ferguson's proposed 'Anglobalisation' of the world was little more than an updated version of American 'modernisation theory', first proposed as an alternative to communism during the Cold War, and now married to revolutionary violence of the kind for which communist regimes had been reviled. It makes for melancholy reading in 2011. But in the first heady year of the global war on terror, easy victories over the ragtag army of the Taliban ignited megalomaniacal fantasies about the 'Rest' across a broad ideological spectrum in Anglo-America, from Ann Coulter arguing that 'we should invade their countries, kill their leaders and convert them to Christianity' to the unctuous 'Empire-Lite' of Michael Ignatieff and the 'liberal imperialism' peddled by Robert Cooper, one of Blair's fly-by-night gurus. 'Islamofascism' seemed as evil as Nazism, Saddam Hussein was another Hitler, a generation-long battle loomed, and invocations of Winston Churchill – 'the greatest', according to Ferguson, 'of all Anglo-Americans', his resolute defence of English-speaking peoples commemorated by a bust in the Bush White House – seemed to stiffen spines all across the Eastern Seaboard.

The reception a writer receives in a favourable political context can be the making of him. This applies particularly well to Ferguson, whose books are known less for their original scholarly contribution than for containing some provocative counterfactuals. In Britain, his bluster about the white man's burden, though largely ignored by academic historians, gained substance from a general rightward shift in political and cultural discourse, which made it imperative for such apostles of public opinion as Andrew Marr to treat Ferguson with reverence. But his apotheosis came in the United States, where – backed by the prestige of Oxbridge and, more important, a successful television series – he became a wise Greek counsellor to many aspiring Romans. He did not have to renounce long-held principles to be elevated to a professorship at Harvard, prime-time punditry on CNN and Fox, and high-altitude wonkfests at Davos and Aspen. He quickly and frictionlessly became the most conspicuous refugee from post-imperial Britain to cheerlead Washington's (and New York's) consensus.

To a reader from the world the British supposedly made, *Empire* belonged recognisably to the tradition of what the Chinese thinker Tang Tiaoding bluntly described in 1903 as 'white people's histories'. Swami Vivekananda, India's most famous nineteenth-century thinker, articulated a widespread moral disapproval of the pith-helmeted missionaries of Western civilisation celebrated by Ferguson:

> Intoxicated by the heady wine of newly acquired power, fearsome like wild animals who see no difference between good and evil, slaves to women, insane in their lust, drenched in alcohol from head to foot, without any norms of ritual conduct, unclean . . . dependent on material things, grabbing other people's land and wealth by hook or by crook . . . the body their self, its appetites their only concern – such is the image of the western demon in Indian eyes.

In 1877, decades before anti-colonial leaders and intellectuals across Asia and Africa developed a systematic political critique of colonialism, the itinerant Muslim activist Jamal al-Din al-Afghani was attacking 'the trap of duplicity' in British accounts of India. The British had invested immense sums in developing a global network of modern communications simply in order, al-Afghani wrote, 'to drain the substance of our wealth and facilitate the means of trade for the inhabitants of the British Isles and extend their sphere of riches'. Two generations of Western historians have essentially confirmed the early Asian and African arguments that the imperatives of 'free trade', whether imposed, as on China, by gunboats, or as on India, by outright occupation, had a devastating effect. The Indian Declaration of Independence in 1930 inadvertently summed up the multifarious damage inflicted on a swathe of subjugated countries from Ottoman Turkey and Egypt to Java:

Village industries, such as hand spinning, have been destroyed . . . and nothing has been substituted, as in other countries, for the crafts thus destroyed.

Customs and currency have been so manipulated as to bring further burdens on the peasantry. British manufactured goods constitute the bulk of our imports. Customs duties betray partiality for British manufacturers, and revenue from them is not used to lessen the burden on the masses but for sustaining a highly extravagant administration. Still more arbitrary has been the manipulation of the exchange ratio, which has resulted in millions being drained away from the country . . . All administrative talent is killed and the masses have to be satisfied with petty village offices and clerkships . . . the system of education has torn us from our moorings.

Ferguson did not entirely ignore the more egregious crimes of imperialism: the slave trade, the treatment of Australian aborigines or the famines that killed tens of millions across Asia. But he offered a robust defence of British motives, which apparently were humanitarian as much as economic. Transporting millions of indentured Asian labourers to far-off colonies (Indians to the Malay Peninsula, Chinese to Trinidad) was terrible, but 'we cannot pretend that this mobilisation of cheap and probably underemployed Asian labour to grow rubber and dig gold had no economic value'. And he challenged the 'fashionable' allegation that 'the British authorities did nothing to relieve the drought-induced famines of the period'. In any case, 'whenever the British were behaving despotically, there was almost always a liberal critique of that behaviour from within British society'. He sounds like the Europeans described by V.S. Naipaul – the grandson of indentured labourers – in *A Bend in the River*, who 'wanted gold and slaves, like everybody else', but also 'wanted statues put up to themselves as people who had done good things for the slaves'.

~

Ferguson's next book, *Colossus: The Rise and Fall of the American Empire*, a selective history of American imperial interventions, showed him to be increasingly concerned with the capability rather than the legitimacy of the American empire. He was convinced that domestic social welfare programmes like Medicare and Medicaid had to be cut drastically in order to build more foreign outposts for jodhpur-clad Americans. But Americans, it turned out, were not rushing to Abercrombie & Fitch to equip themselves for life in the tropics. Some zealous young Republicans in Baghdad's Green Zone were busy dismantling the Iraqi state, but they clearly did not impress Ferguson. 'America's brightest and best', he complained, 'aspire not to govern Mesopotamia but to manage MTV; not to rule the Hejaz but to run a hedge fund.'

'If one adds together the illegal immigrants, the jobless and the convicts,' he argued, 'there is surely ample raw material for a larger American army.' But by 2006, the worst year of the anti-American insurgency, Ferguson was convinced that America was not up to the 'labour-intensive' task of occupying and governing Iraq. Recalling Gibbon for the readers of *Vanity Fair*, he identified some alarmingly diverse portents of the decline and fall of Western civilisation: they included America's dependence on 'Asian central banks and Middle Eastern treasuries' for its wars; Muslim immigrants (Ferguson was an early exponent of 'Eurabia'); feminism, which had caused Europe's demographic decline; and the fact that 'girls no longer play with dolls; they are themselves the dolls, dressed according to the dictates of the fashion industry.' Americans were overweight, while Europeans, turning their back on Christianity and warfare and sponging on the welfare state, were degenerate idlers. 'Endlessly gaming, chatting and chilling with their iPods,' Ferguson wrote, 'the next generation already has a more tenuous connection to "Western civilisation" than most parents appreciate.'

It didn't seem too abrupt when Ferguson abandoned transatlanticism in late 2006, instead investing his intellectual faith and energy in 'Chimerica', a necessary and apt alliance, as he saw it, between China and America, a veritable G2. Throughout his forays into 'provocative' imperial history, Ferguson had maintained his high reputation as an economic historian. 'So vast is America's looming fiscal crisis,' he had written as early as 2004, 'that it is tempting to talk about the fiscal equivalent of the perfect storm – or the perfect earthquake.' But now, awed by the 'rise of China', he saw 'the two halves of Chimerica' as wonderfully 'complementary':

> Profligate West Chimericans cannot get enough of the gadgets mass-produced in the East; they save not a penny of their income and are happy to borrow against their fancy houses. Parsimonious East Chimericans live more humbly and cautiously. They would rather save a third of their own income and lend it to the West Chimericans to fund their gadget habit – and keep East Chimericans in jobs.

This was 'the secular summer of Sino-American symbiosis', Ferguson explained with typical exuberance in early 2007. 'Chimerica, despite its name, is no chimera.'

Speaking at Chatham House in 2011, Ferguson claimed that Chimerica had appealed to him because 'it was a pun', adding that it was not 'true anymore, if it ever was true'. What happened? As he put it, the 'West has suffered a financial crisis that has damaged not only the wealth of the Western world, but perhaps more importantly the legitimacy, the credibility, even the self-esteem of the West.' With the 'Chinese Century' now imminent, and Muslims knocking yet again at the gates of Europe, the important thing for British and American elites is to prepare themselves for a dramatically altered world. 'We are', as he argues in *Civilisation*, 'living through the end of 500 years of Western ascendancy.'

This makes it especially deplorable, in Ferguson's view, that 'major universities have ceased to offer the classic "Western Civ" history course to their undergraduates.' Assaulted by politically correct intellectuals and cultural relativists, who regard 'all civilisations as somehow equal . . . the grand narrative of Western ascent has fallen out of fashion' precisely when it is most needed. 'Maybe,' Ferguson proposes, 'the real threat is posed not by the rise of China, Islam or CO_2 emissions, but by our own loss of faith in the civilisation we inherited from our ancestors.'

Ferguson's outbursts against Britain – 'Get me to the airport,' he told the *Telegraph*, 'I just want to get back to the US' – may have lost him some of his audience among right-wing broadsheets and tabloids in this country. But the anchors of America's cable news networks remain deferential. And Michael Gove, one of the Tories' me-too neocons, has enlisted him to help devise a new history curriculum. For those young men and women willing to swap their iPods for a reassuringly expensive lecture in 'Western Civ', he will also be available periodically at A. C. Grayling's New College of the Humanities. *Civilisation* gives a fair sample of the intellectual and spiritual tonic he would offer there.

Of the various things Tom Buchanan thinks 'go to make civilisation – oh, science and art, and all that', Ferguson is indifferent to the art, mocking Kenneth Clark's TV series, and his '*de haut en bas* manner'. He aims 'to be more down and dirty than high and mighty'. For him, civilisation is best measured by the ability to make 'sustained improvement in the material quality of life', and in this the West has 'patently enjoyed a real and sustained edge over the Rest for most of the previous 500 years'. Ferguson names six 'killer apps' – property rights, competition, science, medicine, the consumer society and the work ethic – as the operating software of Western civilisation that, beginning around 1500, enabled a few small polities at the western end of the Eurasian landmass 'to dominate the rest of the world'.

To explain the contingent, short-lived factors that gave a few countries in Western Europe their advantage over the rest of the world requires a sustained and complex analysis, not one hell-bent on establishing that the West was, and is, best. At the very least, it needs the question to be correctly put. To ask, as Ferguson does, why the West broke through to capitalist modernity and became the originator of globalisation is to assume that this was inevitable, and that it resulted basically from the wonderfulness of the West, not to mention the hopelessness of the East.

Needless to say, most contemporary scholars of global history do not hold the West and the Rest in separate compartments. Far from developing endogenous advantages in splendid isolation from the Rest, Western Europe's 'industrious revolution', which preceded the Industrial Revolution, depended, as Jan de Vries and other historians have shown, on artisanal industries in South and East Asia. Contrary to Ferguson's Hegelian picture of stagnation and decline, China and Japan enjoyed buoyant trade and experienced a consumer boom as late as the eighteenth century. The pioneering work of the Japanese historian Hamashita Takeshi describes a pre-European Asia organised by China's trans-state tributary network, demonstrating that there were many other centres of globalisation in the early modern world apart from those created by Western Europe. In *The Birth of the Modern World, 1780–1914*, which synthesises much recent scholarship on the 'extra-European origins of the modern European and American worlds', C.A. Bayly shows that long-standing Chinese business clans were as important as bourgeois capitalists in Hamburg and New York in spreading world trade across South East Asia. Ferguson should know some of this, since he endorsed Bayly's book when it appeared as 'a masterpiece' that renders 'parochial' all other histories of the nineteenth century.

As in Ferguson's other books, a vast bibliography trails the main text of *Civilisation*, signalling the diligent scholar rather than the populist simplifier. But he suppresses or ignores facts that complicate his picture of the West's *sui generis* efflorescence. Arguing that the Scientific Revolution was 'wholly Eurocentric', he disregards contemporary scholarship about Muslim contributions to Western science, most recently summarised in George Saliba's *Islam and the Making of the European Renaissance*. He prefers the hoary prejudice that Muslim clerics began to shut down rational thought in their societies at the end of the eleventh century. He brusquely dismisses Kenneth Pomeranz's path-breaking book *The Great Divergence*, asserting that 'recent research has demolished the fashionable view that China was economically neck to neck with the West until as recently as 1800.' But he offers no evidence of this fashion-defying research. Given his focus on the ineptitude and collapse of the Ming dynasty, you might think that their successors, the Qing, had for nearly two centuries desperately clung on in a country in irreversible decline rather than, as is the case, presiding over a massive expansion of territory and commercial interests. Each of Ferguson's comparisons and analogies between the West and the Rest, reminiscent of college debating clubs, provokes a counterquestion. The rational Frederick the Great is compared to the orientally despotic and indolent Ottoman Sultan Osman III. Why not, you wonder, to the energetic Tipu Sultan, another Muslim contemporary, who was as keen on military innovation as on foreign trade?

Foregoing cogent argument, Ferguson collects much quiz-friendly information. But he hasn't, to use his own unlovely computer jargon, organised his folders well. Reading about the consumer society, the app that apparently killed communism, you suddenly come across nineteenth-century nationalisms; the benefits of Western medicine segue into the French Revolution. For long periods in the book, the West as well as the Rest disappears under *ex cathedra* pronouncements which often turn out to be mind-bending non sequiturs. A triumphalist claim such as 'even the atheism pioneered in the West is making impressive headway' reveals an ignorance of the strong atheistic strain in

Hindu and Buddhist traditions. It is probably best to ignore the assertion that what the 1960s radicals 'were really after was free love'.

In this gallimaufry, there are useful things. It's true that pre-modern Europe's fierce antagonisms engendered technological innovation at a time when the great empires of Asia were unchallenged, even if this is hardly an idea that should be credited to Charles Murray, a co-author of *The Bell Curve*. Asian leaders and intellectuals, as mute here as in all Ferguson's books, were the keenest analysts of Europe's enhanced capacity to kill, as well as of its innovation of nation-statehood. Mirza Abu Taleb Khan, an Indian Muslim traveller to Europe in 1800, was among the first Asians to point out that, required to fight on sea as well as on land, and to protect their slave plantations in the Caribbean, the British had developed the most sophisticated naval technologies. Fukuzawa Yukichi, the political theorist of Japan's modernisation, lamented in the 1870s that 'we have had too long a period of peace with no intercourse with outside. In the meantime, other countries, stimulated by occasional wars, have invented many new things such as steam trains, steam ships, big guns and small hand guns etc.'

Ferguson does not discuss how many of his apps, imposed on societies historically unprepared for them, could turn literally into killers. The raising of conscript armies, for instance, which helped protect national sovereignty and the expansion of political freedom in the West, could, and more often than not did, strengthen monarchical despotism in the East. Though essential to the growth of Western capitalist economies, notions of absolute property rights turned millions of communitarian peasants in Asia into cheaply hired hands. Modern medicine in the rising West may have been a boon, but it could only be darkly ambiguous in Asia as populations expanded without corresponding economic growth, pushing many into destitution.

As Bayly points out, European and American dominance over 'the world's economies and peoples' meant that, by the end of the nineteenth century, 'a large part of humanity had been converted into long-term losers in the scramble for resources and dignity.' Some of these truths creep into Ferguson's narrative, often while he is arguing something else. 'By 1913,' he writes, 'the world . . . was characterised by a yawning gap between the West and the Rest, which manifested itself in assumptions of white racial superiority and numerous formal and informal impediments to non-white advancement. This was the ultimate global imbalance.' Indeed, and it decided the fate of the many post-colonial nation states whose apparent failure today prompts calls for a new western empire.

Still, Ferguson remains defiantly loyal to his neo-imperialist vision, scoffing at those who can still 'work themselves up into a state of high moral indignation over the misdeeds of the European empires'. 'Misdeeds there certainly were,' he admits and, as in *Empire*, he provides a very selective list that excludes the famines in Bengal, and the extermination of 10 million people in the Congo. Frequently accused since *Empire* of underplaying the dark side of imperialism, Ferguson seems to have come up with a rhetorical strategy: to describe vividly one spectacular instance of brutality – he expends some moral indignation of his own on the slave trade – and then to use this exception to the general rule of imperial benevolence to absolve himself from admitting to the role of imperialism's structural violence in the making of the modern world.

The slave-trading, self-commemorating European conquerors of Asia and Africa, Naipaul writes, 'could do one thing and say something quite different because they had an idea of what they owed to their civilisation'. Ferguson, a retro rather than revisionist historian, tries to summon up some of that old imperial insouciance here. Consequently, his book is immune to the broadly tragic view that every document of civilisation is also a document of barbarism – just as it is to humour and irony.

Even as he deplores the West's decay and dereliction, he sees signs everywhere of its victory: the Resterners are now paying Westerners the ultimate compliment by imitating them. Gratified by the fact that 'more and more human beings eat a Western diet' and 'wear Western clothes', Ferguson is hardly likely to bemoan the cultural homogeneity, or the other viruses – uneven development, environmental degradation – built into the West's operating software. Like his biographical subject, Henry Kissinger, he is mesmerised by the Chinese – in his eyes a thrifty, shrewd people who, in colonising remote African lands and building up massive reserves of capital, seem to borrow from the grand narrative of the West's own ascent. For Kissinger and Ferguson, China is, simultaneously, a serious threat to Western dominance and an opportunity for self-affirmation as it downloads – some might say, pirates or hacks – the West's killer apps.

'The Chinese have got capitalism,' Ferguson exults towards the end of the book. At this point, one hardly expects him to explain whether this is an adequate description of an economy on whose commanding heights a one-party state perches, controlling the movement of capital and running the biggest banks and companies. Writing in 1920, Stoddard was more insightful: Asian peoples are 'not merely adopting', he wrote, 'but adapting, white ideas and methods'. Today these include, in both China and India, some of the harshest aspects of American-style capitalism: the truncation of public services, deunionisation, the fragmenting and lumpenisation of urban working classes, plus the ruthless suppression of the rural poor. But in populous countries you can always find what you seek and Ferguson can't be too worried about these killer apps imported from the contemporary West. He must move on quickly to his next intellectual firework. Did we know that there are more practising Christians in China than in Europe? Ferguson has met many Chinese ready to attest to Protestant Christianity's inexorable rise and its intimate link to China's economic growth. In Wenzhou, the 'Asian Manchester', he comes across a Christian CEO, who strikes him as 'the living embodiment of the link between the spirit of capitalism and the Protestant ethic'.

The reheated Weberism – a sign of Ferguson's nostalgia for the intellectual certainties of the summer of 1914 – turns into another lament for Western civilisation, whose decline is proclaimed everywhere by the fact that the churches are empty, taxes on our wealth are high, the 'thrifty asceticism' of Protestants of yore has been lost, and 'empire has become a dirty word.' 'All we risk being left with', he writes, 'are a vacuous consumer society and a culture of relativism.' And it is with some dark pseudo-Gibbonian speculations about the imminent collapse of the West that *Civilisation* ends.

'Something', Nick Carraway says of Tom Buchanan, 'was making him nibble at the edge of stale ideas as if his sturdy physical egotism no longer nourished his peremptory heart.' 'Western hard power', Ferguson blurts out in *Civilisation*, 'seems to be struggling'; and the book exemplifies a mood, at once swaggering, frustrated, vengeful and despairing, among men of a certain age, class and education on the Upper East Side and the West End. Western civilisation is unlikely to go out of business any time soon, but the neo-imperialist gang might well face redundancy. In that sense, Ferguson's metamorphoses in the last decade – from cheerleader, successively, of empire, Anglobalisation and Chimerica to exponent of collapse theory and retailer of emollient tales about the glorious past – have highlighted broad political and cultural shifts more accurately than his writings have. His next move shouldn't be missed.

2011

2

The Culture of Fear

On Intellectual Islamophobia

Is Europe about to be overrun by Muslims? A number of prominent European and American politicians and journalists seem to think so. The historian Niall Ferguson has predicted that 'a youthful Muslim society to the south and east of the Mediterranean is poised to colonise – the term is not too strong – a senescent Europe.' And according to Christopher Caldwell, an American columnist with the *Financial Times*, whom the *Observer* recently described as a 'bracing, clear-eyed analyst of European pieties', Muslims are already 'conquering Europe's cities, street by street'. So what if Muslims account for only 3 to 4 per cent of the EU's total population of 493 million? In his book *Reflections on the Revolution in Europe: Can Europe Be the Same with Different People in It?* – which was featured on *Start the Week*, excerpted in *Prospect* and commended as 'morally serious' by the *New York Times*, and which has beguiled some liberal opinion makers as well as right-wing blowhards – Caldwell writes, 'Of course minorities can shape countries. They can conquer countries. There were probably fewer Bolsheviks in Russia in 1917 than there are Islamists in Europe today.'

Apparently it's not only Islamist revolutionaries, but also rapidly breeding Muslims who are transforming Europe into 'Eurabia'. The birthrates of Europe's Muslim immigrants are actually falling and converging with national averages, according to a recent survey in the *Financial Times*; but 'advanced' cultures, Caldwell claims in his book, 'have a long track record of underestimating their vulnerability to "primitive" ones'. As the *Daily Telegraph*, quoting Caldwell, asserted last weekend, Britain and the EU have simply ignored the 'demographic time bomb' in their midst. Muslims, Nick Griffin of the BNP once warned, are seducing white girls as part of a plot to take over Britain. Caldwell is also convinced that 'Muslim culture is unusually full of messages laying out the practical advantages of procreation', and, he wonders – though Muslims don't despise Europe as much as Palestinians hate Israel – didn't Yasser Arafat call the wombs of Palestinian women 'the secret weapon' of his cause?

Caldwell stops short of speculating what Europe would or should do to atone for its folly of nurturing a perfidious minority. The Canadian journalist Mark Steyn, whom Martin Amis has hailed as a 'great sayer of the unsayable', does not hesitate to spell it out in his bestselling *America Alone: The End of the World as We Know It*: 'In a democratic age, you can't buck demography – except through civil war. The Serbs figured that out – as other Continentals will in the years ahead: if you can't outbreed the enemy, cull 'em.'

Bruce Bawer, whose book *While Europe Slept: How Radical Islam Is Destroying the West from Within* was nominated for a National Book Critics Circle award, suggests that European officials, who are 'in a position to deport planeloads of people every day', 'could start rescuing Europe tomorrow'. There are now even politicians ready to do the 'unsayable'. The Dutch politician Geert Wilders, whose party was one of the big right-wing winners of June's elections to the European Parliament, proposes expelling millions of Muslims from Europe. A separate ministry for this purpose is advocated by Austria's extreme-right parties, which gained an unprecedented 29 per cent of the popular vote in 2008.

Many European politicians and commentators are reluctant to denounce the headscarf as, in French philosopher André

Glucksmann's description, a 'terrorist operation', or to see the Somali-Dutch polemicist Ayaan Hirsi Ali, presently employed by an American neoconservative think tank, as Islam's Luther. But these sceptics may be, according to Bawer's new book *Surrender: Appeasing Islam, Sacrificing Freedom*, as much the dupes of 'Islamo-fascism' as Europe's multiculturalists, who, Bawer writes, 'might have been invented by Osama bin Laden himself'. At a private conference in Sweden a couple of years ago, I saw some of Anglo-America's leading academics, journalists and columnists denounce Ian Buruma, Timothy Garton Ash and other liberal critics of Hirsi Ali with even more bitter passion than they spent on what Caldwell calls 'the penury, servitude, violence, and mediocrity of Muslim societies worldwide'.

Such rage and contempt was startling. The lone representative of the Muslim world among us, a Turkish scholar, occasionally protested, and was ignored. He later complained in his newspaper column about the 'Islamophobia' that makes his country's accession to the EU all the more arduous. It was hard, then, not to feel the poignancy of Turkish aspirations.

No Muslim country has ever done as much as Turkey to make itself over in the image of a European nation state; the country's westernised elite brutally imposed secularism, among other things, on its devout population of peasants. Despite having taken almost all prescribed routes to Western modernity, Turkey finds that Europe would rather use it as a foil. According to Austria's extreme-right Freedom Party, Christendom's old rival is not welcome in Europe because 'there was no Enlightenment and no Renaissance in Turkey' and 'one of the most important values of Europeans, tolerance, does not count in Turkey.'

The Turks might be forgiven for offering the reminder that Austria was, in living memory, a major collaborator in the Nazi scheme to murder and enslave millions of Europeans. But then, as the historian Tony Judt has pointed out, the modern idea of Europe – the presumed embodiment of democracy, human rights, gender equality and many other good things – conveniently suppresses collective memories of brutal crimes in which almost all European states were complicit.

Genocide during the Second World War, followed by ethnic cleansing, was what finally resolved Europe's long-standing minority 'problem', blasting flat, Judt writes, 'the demographic heath upon which the foundations of a new and less complicated continent were then laid'. In Europe's largest migrations of refugees, some 13 million ethnic Germans fled Poland, Czechoslovakia, Hungary and Romania after the war. The eviction of other ethnic groups (Poles, Czechs, Slovaks) brought many countries closer to fulfilling the Versailles ideal of national homogeneity.

Soon afterwards, the continent began to acquire, in a fit of absentmindedness or optimism, a new foreign population. Western Europe's resurgent post-war economies needed cheap labour, which turned out to be readily available in the parts of Asia and Africa that Europe's tottering old empires had either hastily vacated or still clung on to. France, which had imported tens of thousands of North African labourers to make up for its depleted workforce during the First World War, drew again on the Maghreb, or north-western Africa. Britain depended on its former subjects in India and Pakistan to serve its welfare state. Holland's Muslims came from Morocco and Turkey as well as its old colonies, Indonesia and Suriname. Labour shortages in the early 1960s forced Germany to invite Turks as 'guest workers'. Even Spain in the 1970s was moved to host a large population of Muslims for the first time since the Reconquista.

These immigrants were expected to work hard in their mostly menial jobs and then return to their respective countries. Living in their urban ghettos, they were rarely expected to become full citizens. After the oil crisis of 1973, many European countries tightened restrictions on immigrants. By then, millions of Muslims had decided to settle in Europe, preferring the social segregation and racial discrimination they found in the West to political and economic turmoil at home. They have been joined, since the 1970s, by a second generation of Muslims born in Europe, many of them with bleaker prospects of employment than their parents. Today, about 15–16 million Muslims from families of immigrant origin live in the EU, mostly in the cities.

Surveys and opinion polls repeatedly reveal the average European Muslim to be poor, socially conservative, unhappy about discrimination, but generally content, hopeful about their children – who attend non-religious schools – and eager, like their non-Muslim peers, to get on with their lives. Initially high, birthrates among Muslim communities across Europe are falling as more men and women become literate. Exposure to secular modernity has also weaned many of these immigrants away from traditional faith: only 5 per cent of Muslims in France regularly attend mosques, and elsewhere, too, non-observant 'cultural Muslims' predominate.

Restrictive immigration laws passed since 1973 have generally upheld the conservative idea that, as the German philosopher Carl Schmitt put it, 'a democracy demonstrates its political power by knowing how to refuse or keep at bay something foreign and unequal that threatens its homogeneity.' Denmark now has a law preventing citizens under the age of 24 from securing residence rights for their foreign spouses. Germany appeases anti-Turkish sentiment by requiring migrants from poor countries to pass a language test before joining their spouses in Germany. In 2008, fewer immigrants obtained German citizenship than in any year since unification. European governments, most of which are now centre-right, periodically unfurl the flag of majoritarian nationalism in order to seduce anti-immigrant votes away from extreme-right parties – France's National Front, Austria's Freedom Party, Belgium's Flemish Interest and the British National Party, which have repackaged their foundational anti-Semitism, and now accuse Muslims rather than Jews of secretly conspiring to control the world.

Ordinary Muslims in Europe, who suffer from the demoralisation caused by living as perennial objects of suspicion and contempt, are far from thinking of themselves as a politically powerful, or even cohesive, community, not to speak of conquerors of Europe. So what explains the rash of bestsellers with histrionic titles – *While Europe Slept*, *America Alone*, *The Last Days of Europe*? None of their mostly neocon American authors was previously known for their knowledge of Muslim societies; all of them suffer the handicaps of what the philosopher Charles Taylor, in his introduction to a new collection of scholarly essays entitled *Secularism, Religion and Multicultural Citizenship*, calls 'block thinking', which 'fuses a very varied reality into one indissoluble unity'. The idea of a monolithic 'Islam' in Europe appears an especially pitiable bogey when you regard the varying national origins, linguistic and legal backgrounds, and cultural and religious practices of European Muslims. Many so-called Muslims from secularised Turkey or syncretistic Sindh and Java would be condemned as apostates in Saudi Arabia, whose fundamentalist Wahhabism informs most Western visions of Islam.

Unemployment, discrimination and other generic psychological disorientations of second- or third-generation immigrants make young Muslims in Europe vulnerable to globalised forms of political Islam, many of whose militant versions vend political aphrodisiacs of a restored Islamic community to powerless individuals. But it is a tiny minority that is attracted to or is ready to condone terrorist violence. Not surprisingly, most of these Muslims live in Britain, the European country most tainted by the calamitous 'war on terror' that David Miliband, as well as Barack Obama, now concedes was possible to see as a war on Muslims.

Europe's security and intelligence agencies are demonstrably more effective against Islamist terror groups than they were against many home-grown militant organisations: the murderous attacks on London in July 2005 and Madrid in March 2004 have to be measured against the more numerous and relentless assaults by the IRA in the past and ETA in the present. But the killings of hundreds of thousands of Muslims in Iraq, Afghanistan, Lebanon and Gaza, which are exhaustively reported and not euphemised away as 'collateral damage' by the global Muslim media, have created a general volatility, in which seemingly local acts can, as the Danish cartoon controversy proved, immediately spark a worldwide conflagration. Last month, a German put on trial for abusing an Egyptian pharmacist in a headscarf fatally stabbed his victim in a Dresden court, provoking widespread anti-Europe protests in Egypt.

Stoked by tabloids and opportunist politicians, a general paranoia linking Muslims to extremism has simmered in Europe since 9/11. A mini riot erupted in Birmingham in July 2009, when demonstrators against 'militant Islam' from a group claiming to represent 'English people, from businessmen and women, to football hooligans', clashed with Asian men. Fortunately, the good sense and decency of the great majority of Europeans still prevails in everyday transactions of civil society; this instinctive neighbourly regard may be more effective than the state's many initiatives in keeping the peace among Europe's politically diverse communities.

Nevertheless, Eurabia-mongers from America seem as determined as tabloid hacks to strike terror among white Europeans about their local newsagent or curry house owner. 'If the spread of Pakistani cuisine', Caldwell writes, 'is the single greatest improvement in British public life over the past half-century, it is also worth noting that bombs used for the failed London transport attacks of July 21, 2005, were made from a mix of hydrogen peroxide and chapatti flour.'

Most South Asian cuisine consumed on British high streets hails from India or Bangladesh, rather than Pakistan. Caldwell, however, won't let facts get in the way of the many eagerly consumed chapattis rising up his white British reader's gorge, though a reference to Pakistan 'in the nineteenth century' does make one wonder whether Caldwell can tell his brown folks apart. His grasp of European history, too, seems shaky: Italy, he tells us, is like Sweden in being 'without an important colonial history'. Approvingly quoting Ernest Renan's and Hilaire Belloc's scaremongering about Islam as a threat to 'white civilisation', he seems to be unaware that these two writers also described Jews as inferior 'aliens' in Europe. Remarkably, Caldwell, who is a senior editor with the neoconservative *Weekly Standard*, does not appear to know that Edmund Burke, from whom he derives his book title, had a rather exaggerated reverence for 'Muhammadan law'.

Caldwell does claim to like Islam for its 'primitive' vigour, which he speculates may just revitalise 'drab', materialistic Europe. Indeed, a very 1930s-ish obsession with sexual virility and racial purity runs through *Reflections on the Revolution in Europe*. Quoting from an essay entitled 'White Man, What Now?' by the novelist Matthias Politycki, Caldwell wonders why Europeans today feel so 'contemptible and small, ugly and asexual' before Asians and Africans. Like many fellow neo-conservatives, he seems ultimately less worried about Islamic revolution, which he is probably clever enough to see as no more than a TV-friendly soundbite, than about Europe's cheese-eating surrender monkeys who won't prop up the dwindling power of the US.

Speculating 'why America is hated with such bitterness' in newspaper columns in Europe, Caldwell concludes that Europeans, who have helplessly imitated American culture all along (the 'ethnic women's fiction craze', for instance, developed in America well before Zadie Smith and Monica Ali), finally desire 'emancipation from American tutelage'. This is why most of them opposed the war in Iraq. Even worse: in countries that did line up behind the Bush administration, Europeans encouraged Muslims to be anti-American: 'When Muslims marched in anti-war demonstrations, after all, their secular and Christian fellow citizens marched alongside them.'

The crabby protagonist of Saul Bellow's novel *Mr Sammler's Planet* rages against 'white Protestant America for not keeping better order' in the 1960s and for 'cowardly surrender' to aggressive racial minorities. Sammler, a proto-neocon, believes America's old elites are 'eager in a secret humiliating way to come down and mingle with all the minority mobs and scream against themselves'. Caldwell seems similarly incensed by Europe's self-loathing white liberals, and he is unlikely to have been appeased by the eager complicity shown by Tony Blair, José Aznar, Silvio Berlusconi and other European leaders in supporting the Bush administration's endless wars and tactics of torture and rendition.

'For the first time in centuries,' he writes, 'Europeans are living in a world they did not, for the most part, shape.' More alarmingly, the responsibility for shaping the world is now passing from the US itself; and fear and anxiety ('white man, what now?'), though never explicitly acknowledged, darken every page of Caldwell's book as it tries, like other jeremiads about 'America alone', to boost morale by conjuring up worthy new racial and civilisational enemies.

A more thoughtful conservative than Caldwell could have examined valuably how neo-liberal capitalism, while enriching Europe's transnational elites, has frayed the continent's old cultures and solidarities. In Europe, as in India and China, globalisation has provoked great anxieties about inequality and unemployment, fuelling new xenophobic nationalisms and backlashes against ethnic and religious minorities. The social anthropologist Arjun Appadurai claims in *Fear of Small Numbers: An Essay on the Geography of Anger* that 'minorities are the major site for displacing the anxieties of many states about their own minority or marginality (real or imagined) in a world of a few megastates, of unruly economic flows and compromised sovereignties.'

This at least partly explains why a few hundred women in headscarves incited such fierce passions in a nation state whose geopolitical and cultural insignificance in recent years has only been partly obscured by its hyperactive president, Nicolas

Sarkozy. In *The Politics of the Veil*, the distinguished scholar of gender studies Joan Wallach Scott explains how the banning of a small piece of cloth that covers the head and neck affirmed an 'imagined France', one that was 'secular, individualist and culturally homogeneous' and 'whose reality was secured by excluding dangerous others from the nation'. Scott demonstrates that French Muslim girls, who were directly affected by the law on the *foulard*, were 'strikingly absent from the debates' in France, which were dominated by intellectuals and politicians frantically defining the dangerous 'other' (typically by describing the veil as, in Jacques Attali's words, a 'successor to the Berlin wall').

The veil has now been turned into, Scott writes, a highly charged 'sign of the irreducible difference between Islam and France'. Elsewhere, too, politicians and journalists – self-proclaimed 'liberals' as well as unabashed rightwingers – rhetorically ask whether 'Islam', which allegedly enforces a harsh divine law on all Muslims, is compatible with 'European' values of reason and tolerance, which are supposedly derived from the Enlightenment (or Christianity, as Sarkozy blurted out in 2007, in a revealing breach of republican protocol).

In actuality, the everyday choices of most Muslims in Europe are dictated more by their experience of globalised economies and cultures than by their readings in the Qur'an or sharia. Along with their Hindu and Sikh peers, many Muslims in Europe suffer from the usual pathologies of traditional rural communities transitioning to urban secular cultures: the encounter with social and economic individualism inevitably provokes a crisis of control in nuclear families, as well as such ills as forced marriage, the poor treatment of women and militant sectarianism. However, in practice, millions of Muslims, many of them with bitter experiences of authoritarian states, coexist frictionlessly and gratefully with regimes committed to democracy, freedom of religion and equality before the law.

For many of these Muslim aspirants for full and equal citizenship, the urgent questions are whether the old-style liberalism of

many European nation states, which has traditionally assumed cultural homogeneity, can accommodate minority identity, and whether majority communities in Europe can tolerate expressions of cultural and religious distinctiveness. A part of the secular intellectual priesthood, which cannot survive without its theological opposition between the Enlightenment and Islam, thinks not. In 2004, France's ban on the wearing of headscarves in public schools bluntly clarified that Muslims will have to renounce all signs of their religion in order to become fully French.

This expectation of identity suicide has a rather grim history in enlightened Europe. Voltaire burnished his credentials as a defender of reason and civility with attacks on 'ignorant' and 'barbarous' Jews who, as slaves to their scripture, were, 'all of them, born with raging fanaticism in their hearts'. (The Nazis put together a sizeable anthology of Voltaire's rants against Jews.) Accused of mistreating their women and proliferating with devious rapidity, and goaded to abandon their religious and cultural baggage, many Jews in the nineteenth century paid an even higher cost of 'integration' than that confronting Muslims today in France.

As it turned out, those Jews who suppressed the Torah and Talmud and underwent drastic embourgeoisement became even more vulnerable to malign prejudice in post-Enlightenment Europe's secular nation states. The persecution of Alfred Dreyfus in France convinced Theodore Herzl, the creator of modern Zionism, that 'the Jew who tries to adapt himself to his environment, to speak its languages, to think its thoughts' would remain a potentially treacherous 'alien' in the secular West. Reporting in the 1920s on Jewish communities exposed to a particularly vicious recrudescence of anti-Semitism, the novelist Joseph Roth denounced assimilation as a dangerous illusion, blaming its failure on the 'habitual bias that governs the actions, decisions, and opinions of the average western European'.

Roth, who trusted Europe's old 'fear of God' more than its 'so-called modern humanism', bluntly questioned the 'civilising missions' of European empires in Asia and Africa in a preface he wrote to his book in 1937: 'What is it', he asked, 'that allows European states to go spreading civilisation and ethics in foreign parts but not at home?' Joan Wallach Scott's account of France's colonial history reveals that violent prejudice against religious and racial 'others' was also an intrinsic part of spreading European civilisation and ethics abroad. The veil, fixed in the nineteenth century by the French as a symbol of Islam's primitive backwardness, was used to justify the brutal pacification of North African Muslims and to exclude them from full citizenship. Geoffrey Brahm Levey and Tariq Modood, the editors of *Secularism, Religion and Multicultural Citizenship*, write: 'How Muslims are perceived today is connected to how they have been perceived and treated by European empires and their racial hierarchies.'

Meanwhile, as colonialist stereotypes again proliferate, second- and third-generation Muslim women creatively use their head coverings in their own passage to modernity. In *Another Cosmopolitanism*, the political philosopher Seyla Benhabib describes the bold actions of three French girls who in 1989 consciously risked expulsion by wearing headscarves to school:

> They used the symbol of the home to gain entry into the public sphere by retaining the modesty required of Islam in covering their heads; yet at the same time, they left the home to become public actors in a civil public space in which they defied the state.

Liberal spaces within Europe have brought many more Muslim women out of their old confinements. Benhabib asserts that these women, who 'struggle at first to retain their traditional and given identities against the pressures of the state', then go on to engage and contest their Islamic traditions. As Europe's own passage from tradition showed, this necessary reconfiguration is not the work of a day. It requires the practices and institutions of European citizenship to grow more rather than less flexible.

In historic terms, Muslims are a recent presence in Europe, especially when compared to the minorities in different parts of the continent – Jewish, Italian, Portuguese and black – who were once feared to be unassimilable. Their initial position as barely tolerated 'temporary workers' was never likely to create the conditions for quick integration. Muslims from a young, globalised and highly political generation are now poised to enter the public spheres open to them, or to embrace extremism, or, like many of their parents, to retreat into passive resentment. But these choices in turn depend on how quickly and readily their 'hosts' – ordinary Europeans as well as their governments – will make them feel at home. Strident invocations of the Enlightenment or some other historically and eternally fixed essence of Europe seem increasingly symptoms of intellectual lag and cultural defensiveness. Multi-ethnic Europe is an immutable fact, and needs, appropriately, a more inclusive, open-ended identity, one derived more from its pluralistic and relatively peaceful present, and supranational future, than from its brutishly nationalist and imperialist past. Writing in 1937 about the minority then most despised in Europe, Joseph Roth predicted that 'Jews will only attain complete equality, and the dignity of external freedom, once their "host nations" have attained their own inner freedom, as well as the dignity conferred by sympathy for the plight of others'. This proved to be too much to ask of Europe in 1937. But the moral challenge has not gone away – civilisation remains an ideal rather than an irreversible achievement – and the dangers of leaving it unmet are incalculable.

2009

3

The Religion of Whiteness

How to Remember the First World War

'Today on the Western Front,' the German sociologist Max Weber wrote in September 1917, there 'stands a dross of African and Asiatic savages and all the world's rabble of thieves and lumpens.' Weber was referring to the millions of Indian, African, Arab, Chinese and Vietnamese soldiers and labourers, who were then fighting with British and French forces in Europe, as well as in several ancillary theatres of the First World War.

Faced with manpower shortages, British imperialists had recruited up to 1.4 million Indian soldiers. France enlisted nearly 500,000 troops from its colonies in Africa and Indo-China. Nearly 400,000 African Americans were also inducted into US forces. The First World War's truly unknown soldiers are these non-white combatants.

Ho Chi Minh, who spent much of the war in Europe, denounced what he saw as the press-ganging of subordinate peoples. Before the start of the Great War, Ho wrote, they were seen as 'nothing but dirty Negroes . . . good for no more than pulling rickshaws'. But when Europe's slaughter machines needed 'human fodder', they were called into service. Other anti-imperialists, such as Mohandas Gandhi and W.E.B. Du Bois, vigorously supported the war aims of their white overlords, hoping to secure dignity for their compatriots in the aftermath. But they did not realise what Weber's remarks revealed: that Europeans had quickly come to fear and hate physical proximity to their non-white subjects – their 'new-caught sullen peoples', as Kipling called colonised Asians and Africans in his 1899 poem 'The White Man's Burden'.

These colonial subjects remain marginal in popular histories of the war. They also go largely uncommemorated by the hallowed rituals of Remembrance Day. The ceremonial walk to the Cenotaph at Whitehall by all major British dignitaries, the two minutes of silence broken by the last post, the laying of poppy wreaths and the singing of the national anthem – all of these uphold the First World War as Europe's stupendous act of self-harm. For the past century, the war has been remembered as a great rupture in modern Western civilisation, an inexplicable catastrophe that highly civilised European powers sleepwalked into after the 'long peace' of the nineteenth century – a catastrophe whose unresolved issues provoked yet another calamitous conflict between liberal democracy and authoritarianism, in which the former finally triumphed, returning Europe to its proper equilibrium.

With more than 8 million dead and more than 21 million wounded, the war was the bloodiest in European history until that second conflagration on the continent ended in 1945. War memorials in Europe's remotest villages, as well as the cemeteries of Verdun, the Marne, Passchendaele and the Somme, enshrine a heartbreakingly extensive experience of bereavement. In many books and films, the pre-war years appear as an age of prosperity and contentment in Europe, with the summer of 1913 featuring as the last golden summer.

But today, as racism and xenophobia return to the centre of Western politics, it is time to remember that the background to the First World War was decades of racist imperialism whose consequences still endure. It is something that is not remembered much, if at all, on Remembrance Day.

At the time of the First World War, all Western powers upheld a racial hierarchy built around a shared project of territorial expansion. In 1917, the US president, Woodrow Wilson, baldly stated his intention 'to keep the white race strong against the yellow' and to preserve 'white civilisation and its domination of the planet'. Eugenicist ideas of racial selection were everywhere in the mainstream, and the anxiety expressed in papers like the *Daily Mail*, which worried about white women coming into contact with 'natives who are worse than brutes when their passions are aroused', was widely shared across the West. Anti-miscegenation laws existed in most US states. In the years leading up to 1914, prohibitions on sexual relations between European women and black men (though not between European men and African women) were enforced across European colonies in Africa. The presence of the 'dirty Negroes' in Europe after 1914 seemed to be violating a firm taboo.

In May 1915, a scandal erupted when the *Daily Mail* printed a photograph of a British nurse standing behind a wounded Indian soldier. Army officials tried to withdraw white nurses from hospitals treating Indians, and disbarred the latter from leaving the hospital premises without a white male companion. The outrage when France deployed soldiers from Africa (a majority of them from the Maghreb) in its post-war occupation of Germany was particularly intense and more widespread. Germany had also fielded thousands of African soldiers while trying to hold on to its colonies in East Africa, but it had not used them in Europe, or indulged in what the German foreign minister (and former governor of Samoa), Wilhelm Solf, called 'racially shameful use of coloureds'.

'These savages are a terrible danger,' a joint declaration of the German national assembly warned in 1920, to 'German women'. Writing *Mein Kampf* in the 1920s, Adolf Hitler would describe African soldiers on German soil as a Jewish conspiracy aimed to topple white people 'from their cultural and political ⁣ights'. The Nazis, who were inspired by American innova- ⁣s in racial hygiene, would in 1937 forcibly sterilise hundreds ⁣ldren fathered by African soldiers. Fear and hatred of ⁣niggers' (as Weber called them) on German soil was

47

not confined to Germany, or to the political right. The Pope protested against their presence, and an editorial in the *Daily Herald*, a British socialist newspaper, in 1920 was titled 'Black Scourge in Europe'.

This was the prevailing global racial order, built around an exclusionary notion of whiteness and buttressed by imperialism, pseudo-science and the ideology of social Darwinism. In our own time, the steady erosion of the inherited privileges of race has destabilised Western identities and institutions – and it has unveiled racism as an enduringly potent political force, empowering volatile demagogues in the heart of the modern West.

Today, as white supremacists feverishly build transnational alliances, it becomes imperative to ask, as Du Bois did in 1910, 'What is whiteness that one should so desire it?' As we remember the first global war, it must be remembered against the background of a project of Western global domination – one that was shared by all of the war's major antagonists. The First World War, in fact, marked the moment when the violent legacies of imperialism in Asia and Africa returned home, exploding into self-destructive carnage in Europe. And it seems ominously significant on 2017's Remembrance Day, when the potential for large-scale mayhem in the West seems greater than at any other time in its long peace since 1945.

When historians discuss the origins of the Great War, they usually focus on rigid alliances, military timetables, imperialist rivalries, arms races and German militarism. The war, they repeatedly tell us, was the seminal calamity of the twentieth century – Europe's original sin, which enabled even bigger eruptions of savagery such as the Second World War and the Holocaust. An extensive literature on the war, literally tens of thousands of books and scholarly articles, largely dwells on the western front and the impact of the mutual butchery on Britain, France and Germany – and, significantly, on the metropolitan cores of these imperial powers rather than their peripheries. In this orthodox narrative, which is punctuated by the Russian Revolution and the Balfour declaration in 1917, the war begins with the 'guns of August' in 1914, and exultantly patriotic crowds across Europe send soldiers off to a bloody stalemate in the trenches. Peace arrives with the Armistice of 11 November 1918, only to be tragically compromised by the Treaty of Versailles in 1919, which sets the stage for another world war.

In one predominant but highly ideological version of European history – popularised since the Cold War – the world wars, together with fascism and communism, are simply monstrous aberrations in the universal advance of liberal democracy and freedom. In many ways, however, it is the decades after 1945 – when Europe, deprived of its colonies, emerged from the ruins of two cataclysmic wars – that increasingly seem exceptional. Amid a general exhaustion with militant and collectivist ideologies in Western Europe, the virtues of democracy – above all, the respect for individual liberties – seemed clear. The practical advantages of a reworked social contract, and a welfare state, were also obvious. But neither these decades of relative stability, nor the collapse of communist regimes in 1989, were a reason to assume that human rights and democracy were rooted in European soil.

Instead of remembering the First World War in a way that flatters our contemporary prejudices, we should recall what Hannah Arendt pointed out in *The Origins of Totalitarianism* – one of the West's first major reckonings with Europe's grievous twentieth-century experience of wars, racism and genocide. Arendt observes that it was Europeans who initially reordered 'humanity into master and slave races' during their conquest and exploitation of much of Asia, Africa and America. This debasing hierarchy of races was established because the promise of equality and liberty at home required imperial expansion abroad in order to be even partially fulfilled. We tend to forget that imperialism, with its promise of land, food and raw materials, was widely seen in the late nineteenth century as crucial to national progress and prosperity. Racism was – and is – more than an ugly prejudice, something to be eradicated through legal and social proscription. It involved real attempts to solve, through exclusion and degradation, the problems of establishing political order, and pacifying the disaffected, in societies roiled by rapid social and economic change.

In the early twentieth century, the popularity of social Darwinism had created a consensus that nations should be seen similarly to biological organisms, which risked extinction or decay if they failed to expel alien bodies and achieve 'living space' for their own citizens. Pseudo-scientific theories of biological difference between races posited a world in which all races were engaged in an international struggle for wealth and power. Whiteness became 'the new religion', as Du Bois witnessed, offering security amid disorienting economic and technological shifts, and a promise of power and authority over a majority of the human population.

The resurgence of these supremacist views today in the West – alongside the far more widespread stigmatisation of entire populations as culturally incompatible with white Western peoples – should suggest that the First World War was not, in fact, a profound rupture with Europe's own history. Rather it was, as Liang Qichao, China's foremost modern intellectual, was already insisting in 1918, a 'mediating passage that connects the past and the future'.

The liturgies of Remembrance Day, and evocations of the beautiful long summer of 1913, deny both the grim reality that preceded the war and the way it has persisted into the twenty-first century. Our complex task during the war's centenary is to identify the ways in which that past has infiltrated our present, and how it threatens to shape the future: how the terminal weakening of white civilisation's domination, and the assertiveness of previously sullen peoples, has released some very old tendencies and traits in the West.

Nearly a century after the First World War ended, the experiences and perspectives of its non-European actors and observers remain largely obscure. Most accounts of the war uphold it as an essentially European affair: one in which the continent's long peace is shattered by four years of carnage, and a long tradition of Western rationalism is perverted.

Relatively little is known about how the war accelerated political struggles across Asia and Africa; how Arab and Turkish nationalists, and Indian and Vietnamese anti-colonial activists, found new opportunities in it; or how, while destroying old empires in Europe, the war turned Japan into a menacing imperialist power in Asia.

A broad account of the war that is attentive to political conflicts outside Europe can clarify the hyper-nationalism today of many Asian and African ruling elites, most conspicuously the Chinese regime, which presents itself as avengers of China's century-long humiliation by the West.

Recent commemorations have made greater space for the non-European soldiers and battlefields of the First World War: altogether more than 4 million non-white men were mobilised into European and American armies, and fighting happened in places very remote from Europe – from Siberia and East Asia to the Middle East, sub-Saharan Africa, and even the South Pacific islands. In Mesopotamia, Indian soldiers formed a majority of Allied manpower throughout the war. Neither Britain's occupation of Mesopotamia nor its successful campaign in Palestine would have occurred without Indian assistance. Sikh soldiers even helped the Japanese to evict Germans from their Chinese colony of Qingdao.

Scholars have started to pay more attention to the nearly 140,000 Chinese and Vietnamese contract labourers hired by the British and French governments to maintain the war's infrastructure, mostly digging trenches. We know more about how interwar Europe became host to a multitude of anti-colonial movements; the East Asian expatriate community in Paris at one point included Zhou Enlai, later the premier of China, as well as Ho Chi Minh. Cruel mistreatment, in the form of segregation and slave labour, was the fate of many of these Asians and Africans in Europe. Deng Xiaoping, who arrived in France just after the war, later recalled 'the humiliations' inflicted upon fellow Chinese by 'the running dogs of capitalists'.

But in order to grasp the current homecoming of white supremacism in the West, we need an even deeper history – one that shows how whiteness became, in the late nineteenth century, the assurance of individual identity and dignity, as well as the basis of military and diplomatic alliances.

Such a history would show that the global racial order in the century preceding 1914 was one in which it was entirely natural for 'uncivilised' peoples to be exterminated, terrorised, imprisoned, ostracised or radically re-engineered. Moreover, this entrenched system was not something incidental to the First World War, with no connections to the vicious way it was fought or to the brutalisation that made possible the horrors of the Holocaust. Rather, the extreme, lawless and often gratuitous violence of modern imperialism eventually boomeranged on its originators.

In this new history, Europe's long peace is revealed as a time of unlimited wars in Asia, Africa and the Americas. These colonies emerge as the crucible where the sinister tactics of Europe's brutal twentieth-century wars – racial extermination, forced population transfers, contempt for civilian lives – were first forged. Contemporary historians of German colonialism (an expanding field of study) try to trace the Holocaust back to the mini-genocides Germans committed in their African colonies in the 1900s, where some key ideologies, such as Lebensraum, were also nurtured. But it is too easy to conclude, especially from an Anglo-American perspective, that Germany broke from the norms of civilisation to set a new standard of barbarity, strong-arming the rest of the world into an age of extremes. For there were deep continuities in the imperialist practices and racial assumptions of European and American powers.

Indeed, the mentalities of the Western powers converged to a remarkable degree during the high noon of 'whiteness' – what Du Bois, answering his own question about this highly desirable condition, memorably defined as 'the ownership of the Earth for ever and ever'. For example, the German colonisation of South West Africa, which was meant to solve the problem of overpopulation, was often assisted by the British, and all major Western powers amicably sliced and shared the Chinese melon in the late nineteenth century. Any tensions that arose between those dividing the booty of Asia and Africa were defused largely peacefully, if at the expense of Asians and Africans.

This is because colonies had, by the late nineteenth century, come to be widely seen as indispensable relief valves for domestic socio-economic pressures. Cecil Rhodes put the case for them with exemplary clarity in 1895 after an encounter with angry unemployed men in London's East End. Imperialism, he declared, was a

> solution for the social problem, ie in order to save the 40 million inhabitants of the United Kingdom from a bloody civil war, we colonial statesmen must acquire new lands to settle the surplus population, to provide new markets for the goods produced in the factories and mines.

In Rhodes's view, 'if you want to avoid civil war, you must become imperialists.'

Rhodes's scramble for Africa's gold fields helped trigger the second Boer War, during which the British, interning Afrikaner women and children, brought the term 'concentration camp' into ordinary parlance. By the end of the war in 1902, it had become a 'commonplace of history', J.A. Hobson wrote, that 'governments use national animosities, foreign wars and the glamour of empire-making in order to bemuse the popular mind and divert rising resentment against domestic abuses.'

With imperialism opening up a 'panorama of vulgar pride and crude sensationalism', ruling classes everywhere tried harder to 'imperialise the nation', as Arendt wrote. This project to 'organise the nation for the looting of foreign territories and the permanent degradation of alien peoples' was quickly advanced through the newly established tabloid press. The *Daily Mail*, right from its inception in 1896, stoked vulgar pride in being white, British and superior to the brutish natives – just as it does today.

At the end of the war, Germany was stripped of its colonies and accused by the victorious imperial powers, entirely without irony, of ill-treating its natives in Africa. But such judgements, still made today to distinguish a 'benign' British and American imperialism from the German, French, Dutch and Belgian versions, try to suppress the vigorous synergies of racist imperialism. Marlow, the narrator of Joseph Conrad's *Heart of Darkness*, is clear-sighted about them: 'All Europe contributed to the making of Kurtz,' he says. And to the newfangled modes of exterminating the brutes, he might have added.

In 1920, a year after condemning Germany for its crimes against Africans, the British devised aerial bombing as routine policy in their new Iraqi possession – the forerunner to today's decade-long bombing and drone campaigns in West and South Asia. 'The Arab and Kurd now know what real bombing means,' a 1924 report by a Royal Air Force officer put it. 'They now know that within 45 minutes a full-sized village . . . can be practically wiped out and a third of its inhabitants killed or injured.' This officer was Arthur 'Bomber' Harris, who in the Second World War unleashed the firestorms of Hamburg and Dresden, and whose pioneering efforts in Iraq helped German theorising in the 1930s about *der totale Krieg* (total war).

It is often proposed that Europeans were indifferent to or absent-minded about their remote imperial possessions, and that only a few dyed-in-the-wool imperialists like Rhodes, Kipling and Lord Curzon cared enough about them. This makes racism seem like a minor problem that was aggravated by the arrival of Asian and African immigrants in post-1945 Europe. But the frenzy of jingoism with which Europe plunged into a bloodbath in 1914 speaks of a belligerent culture of imperial domination, a macho language of racial superiority, that had come to bolster national and individual self-esteem.

Italy actually joined Britain and France on the Allied side in 1915 in a fit of popular empire-mania (and promptly plunged into fascism after its imperialist cravings went unslaked). Italian writers and journalists, as well as politicians and businessmen, had lusted after imperial power and glory since the late nineteenth century. Italy had fervently scrambled for Africa, only to be ignominiously routed by Ethiopia in 1896. (Mussolini would avenge that in 1935 by dousing Ethiopians with poison gas.) In 1911, it saw an opportunity to detach Libya from the Ottoman Empire. Coming after previous setbacks, its assault on the country, green-lighted by both Britain and France, was vicious and loudly cheered at home. News of the Italians' atrocities, which included the first bombing from air in history, radicalised many Muslims across Asia and Africa. But public opinion in Italy remained implacably behind the imperial gamble.

Germany's own militarism, commonly blamed for causing Europe's death spiral between 1914 and 1918, seems less extraordinary when we consider that, from the 1880s, many Germans in politics, business and academia, and such powerful lobby groups as the Pan-German League (Max Weber was briefly a member), had exhorted their rulers to achieve the imperial status of Britain and France. Furthermore, all Germany's military engagements from 1871 to 1914 occurred outside Europe. These included punitive expeditions in the African colonies and one ambitious foray in 1900 in China, where Germany joined seven other European powers in a retaliatory expedition against young Chinese who had rebelled against Western domination of the Middle Kingdom.

Dispatching German troops to Asia, the kaiser presented their mission as racial vengeance: 'Give no pardon and take no prisoners,' he said, urging the soldiers to make sure that 'no Chinese will ever again even dare to look askance at a

German'. The crushing of the 'Yellow Peril' (a phrase coined in the 1890s) was more or less complete by the time the Germans arrived. Nevertheless, between October 1900 and spring 1901 the Germans launched dozens of raids in the Chinese countryside that became notorious for their intense brutality.

One of the volunteers for the disciplinary force was Lt Gen. Lothar von Trotha, who had made his reputation in Africa by slaughtering natives and incinerating villages. He called his policy 'terrorism', adding that it 'can only help' to subdue the natives. In China, he despoiled Ming graves and presided over a few killings, but his real work lay ahead, in German South West Africa (contemporary Namibia), where an anti-colonial uprising broke out in January 1904. In October of that year, Von Trotha ordered that members of the Herero community, including women and children, who had already been defeated militarily, were to be shot on sight and those escaping death were to be driven into the Omaheke Desert, where they would be left to die from exposure. An estimated 60,000–70,000 Herero people, out of a total of approximately 80,000, were eventually killed, and many more died in the desert from starvation. A second revolt against German rule in South West Africa by the Nama people led to the demise, by 1908, of roughly half of their population.

Such proto-genocides became routine during the last years of European peace. Running the Congo Free State as his personal fief from 1885 to 1908, King Leopold II of Belgium reduced the local population by half, sending as many as 8 million Africans to an early death. The American conquest of the Philippines between 1898 and 1902, to which Kipling dedicated 'The White Man's Burden', took the lives of more than 200,000 civilians. The death toll perhaps seems less startling when one considers that 26 of the 30 US generals in the Philippines had fought in wars of annihilation against Native Americans at home. One of them, Brigadier General Jacob H. Smith, explicitly stated in his order to the troops, 'I want no prisoners. I wish you to kill and burn. The more you kill and burn the better it will please me.' In a Senate hearing on the atrocities in the Philippines, General Arthur MacArthur (father of Douglas) referred to the 'magnificent Aryan peoples' he belonged to and the 'unity of the race' he felt compelled to uphold.

The modern history of violence shows that ostensibly staunch foes have never been reluctant to borrow murderous ideas from one another. To take only one instance, the American elite's ruthlessness with blacks and Native Americans greatly impressed the earliest generation of German liberal imperialists, decades before Hitler also came to admire the US's unequivocally racist policies of nationality and immigration. The Nazis sought inspiration from Jim Crow legislation in the US South, which makes Charlottesville, Virginia, a fitting recent venue for the unfurling of swastika banners and chants of 'blood and soil'.

In light of this shared history of racial violence, it seems odd that we continue to portray the First World War as a battle between democracy and authoritarianism, as a seminal and unexpected calamity. The Indian writer Aurobindo Ghose was one among many anti-colonial thinkers who predicted, even before the outbreak of war, that 'vaunting, aggressive, dominant Europe' was already under 'a sentence of death', awaiting 'annihilation' – much as Liang Qichao could see, in 1918, that the war would prove to be a bridge connecting Europe's past of imperial violence to its future of merciless fratricide.

These shrewd assessments were not oriental wisdom or African clairvoyance. Many subordinate peoples simply realised, well before Arendt published *The Origins of Totalitarianism* in 1951, that peace in the metropolitan West depended too much on outsourcing war to the colonies.

The experience of mass death and destruction, suffered by most Europeans only after 1914, was first widely known in Asia and Africa, where land and resources were forcefully usurped, economic and cultural infrastructure was systematically destroyed, and entire populations were eliminated with the help of up-to-date bureaucracies and technologies. Europe's equilibrium was parasitic for too long on disequilibrium elsewhere.

In the end, Asia and Africa could not remain a safely remote venue for Europe's wars of aggrandisement in the late nineteenth and twentieth centuries. Populations in Europe eventually suffered the great violence that had long been inflicted on Asians and Africans. As Arendt warned, violence administered for the sake of power 'turns into a destructive principle that will not stop until there is nothing left to violate'.

In our own time, nothing better demonstrates this ruinous logic of lawless violence, which corrupts both public and private morality, than the heavily racialised war on terror. It presumes a subhuman enemy who must be 'smoked out' at home and abroad – and it has licensed the use of torture and extrajudicial execution, even against Western citizens.

But, as Arendt predicted, its failures have only produced an even greater dependence on violence, a proliferation of undeclared wars and new battlefields, a relentless assault on civil rights at home – and an exacerbated psychology of domination, presently manifest in Donald Trump's threats to trash the nuclear deal with Iran and unleash on North Korea 'fire and fury like the world has never seen'.

It was always an illusion to suppose that 'civilised' peoples could remain immune, at home, to the destruction of morality and law in their wars against barbarians abroad. But that illusion, long cherished by the self-styled defenders of Western civilisation, has now been shattered, with racist movements ascendant in Europe and the US, often applauded by the white supremacist in the White House, who is making sure there is nothing left to violate.

The white nationalists have junked the old rhetoric of liberal internationalism, the preferred language of the Western political and media establishment for decades. Instead of claiming to make the world safe for democracy, they nakedly assert the cultural unity of the white race against an existential threat posed by swarthy foreigners, whether these are citizens, immigrants, refugees, asylum seekers or terrorists.

But the global racial order that for centuries bestowed power, identity, security and status on its beneficiaries has finally begun to break down. Not even war with China, or ethnic cleansing in the West, will restore to whiteness its ownership of the Earth for ever and ever. Regaining imperial power and glory has already proven to be a treacherous escapist fantasy – devastating the Middle East and parts of Asia and Africa while bringing terrorism back to the streets of Europe and America – not to mention ushering Britain towards Brexit.

No rousing quasi-imperialist ventures abroad can mask the chasms of class and education, or divert the masses, at home. Consequently, the social problem appears insoluble; acrimoniously polarised societies seem to verge on the civil war that Rhodes feared; and, as Brexit and Trump show, the capacity for self-harm has grown ominously.

This is also why whiteness, first turned into a religion during the economic and social uncertainty that preceded the violence of 1914, is the world's most dangerous cult today. Racial supremacy has been historically exercised through colonialism, slavery, segregation, ghettoisation, militarised border controls and mass incarceration. It has now entered its last and most desperate phase with Trump in power.

We can no longer discount the 'terrible probability' that James Baldwin once described: that the winners of history,

> struggling to hold on to what they have stolen from their captives, and unable to look into their mirror, will precipitate a chaos throughout the world which, if it does not bring life on this planet to an end, will bring about a racial war such as the world has never seen.

Sane thinking would require, at the very least, an examination of the history – and stubborn persistence – of racist imperialism:

a reckoning that Germany alone among Western powers has attempted.

Certainly the risk of not confronting our true history has never been as clear as on this Remembrance Day. If we continue to evade it, historians a century from now may once again wonder why the West sleepwalked, after a long peace, into its biggest calamity yet.

2018

4

The Personal as Political

On Salman Rushdie

'Politics and literature', Salman Rushdie wrote in 1984, in what now seems an innocent time, 'do mix, are inextricably mixed, and that . . . mixture has consequences.' Criticising George Orwell for having advocated political quietism to writers, Rushdie asserted that 'we are all irradiated by history, we are radioactive with history and politics', and that, 'in this world without quiet corners, there can be no easy escapes from history, from hullabaloo, from terrible, unquiet fuss.'

Five years later, his novel *The Satanic Verses* would be abruptly inserted into a series of ongoing domestic and international confrontations in the West and in Muslim countries. Sentenced to death by an Iranian theocrat, Rushdie himself would embody the perils of mixing politics and literature in an interconnected and volatile world, where, as Paul Valéry once warned, 'nothing can ever happen again without the whole world's taking a hand' and where 'no one will ever be able to predict or circumscribe the almost immediate consequences of any undertaking whatever'.

In his new memoir *Joseph Anton*, which describes his life in hiding for more than a decade, Rushdie claims that *The Satanic Verses* was his 'least political book'. It was 'an artistic engagement with the phenomenon of revelation', albeit from the perspective of an 'unbeliever', but 'a proper one nonetheless. How could that be thought offensive?' But then authorial intentions barely seemed to matter to readers bringing to the book their own particular backgrounds, world views and prejudices.

No one among Rushdie's early readers in Europe and America seems to have suspected that parts of the novel constituted, as Eliot Weinberger wrote in 1989, an 'all-out parodic assault on the basic tenets of Islam'. A pre-publication review in the Indian newsweekly *India Today* revealed that Rushdie had irreverently rewritten the life of the Prophet, the paradigmatic figure of virtue for all Muslims, naming him Mahound, the term used to identify him as a devil in medieval Christian caricature, and placing his twelve wives in a brothel. Rushdie claimed in the accompanying interview that the image out of which his book grew was of the Prophet 'going to the mountain and not being able to tell the difference between the angel and the devil'.

Responding to the coverage in *India Today*, some self-proclaimed leaders of Indian Muslims demanded a ban on *The Satanic Verses*. The Indian government rashly obliged, prohibiting the novel's importation (though copies were already in circulation). 'You own the present,' Rushdie appealed unsuccessfully to the Indian prime minister, Rajiv Gandhi, 'but the centuries belong to art.' The following month South Africa proscribed the book. Nearly 70 per cent of Bolton's Muslim population turned up for Britain's first major demonstration against the book. Most of the Muslims protesting against the book had not read it; but many of those who had were no less 'transfixed with fear, anger and hatred', as the writer Ziauddin Sardar, himself a critic of Islamic fundamentalism, confessed.

Rushdie's exemplary record of anti-racism amounted to little as demonstrators in Bradford ceremonially burnt a copy of *The Satanic Verses*. As with the 2012 film *Innocence of Muslims*, news of the novel's alleged insult to Islam travelled speedily to politically combustible regions. Some Kashmiris in Srinagar, fighting a corrupt and brutal Indian rule, found in the book another pretext to ventilate their rage, and a differently motivated crowd of Pakistani protesters attacked the American Center in Islamabad, claiming the first of many lives consumed by a fast-spreading global wildfire. No one, however, weaponised the novel with more devastating effect than Iran's chief cleric, then bloodily consolidating his young theocracy and Iran's claims to global Muslim leadership after a catastrophic eight-year war with Iraq.

Khomeini's unconscionable fatwa, though immediately condemned by most critics of *The Satanic Verses*, widened the already great chasm of perception and historical memory between white Westerners and the Muslim inhabitants of former Western empires. In Britain, it became another pretext for rants about Muslim barbarism, and fresh assaults on the straw man of 'multiculturalism'. 'We fell for the idea', Michael Ignatieff later admitted, speaking for many liberal intellectuals, not to mention quasi-racist right-wingers, 'that the ayatollah was speaking for the whole faith.' In this atmosphere of 'anti-Muslim feeling', as Bhikhu Parekh described it, most Muslims were seen as fundamentalists or 'illiterate peasants preferring the sleep of superstition to liberal light, and placed outside civilised discourse'.

Christopher Hitchens's gloss on Islam was not untypical: 'the very word is like the echo of a forehead knocking repeatedly on the floor, while the buttocks are proffered to the empty, unfeeling sky.' Not surprisingly, as Malise Ruthven wrote, 'Muslims in Britain and abroad' who already felt the sharp edge of the 'power of the west' responded 'to *The Satanic Verses* as an assault on their collective cultural identity'.

Simple assertions of the principle of free speech did not persuade those Muslims who were aware of laws that protected Christians from blasphemy. Edward Said, while correctly defending Rushdie's right to untrammelled expression, tried to ventriloquise the Muslim sense of hurt and bafflement: 'Why must a Muslim, who could be defending and sympathetically interpreting us, now present us so roughly, so expertly and so disrespectfully to an audience already primed to excoriate our traditions, reality, history, religion, language, and origins?' But the question suffered from many misunderstandings about Rushdie's position and role as an expatriate novelist from a former imperial possession.

Like many writers of non-Western backgrounds in the West, Rushdie had suffered the ambiguous fate of being hastily appointed as a representative and spokesperson of India, South Asia, the 'Third World', multiculturalism, the immigrant condition – whatever seemed alien and incomprehensible to the white majority. In reality, there was little in common between Rushdie, an atheistic, Cambridge-educated upper-class intellectual from Bombay, and the devout guest worker from Anatolia (representative of the mostly working-class Muslims of rural origins who had been imported to service Europe's post-war economies), or the Pakistani trade unionist chased out by the torturers of Zia ul-Haq, or the CIA-backed radical Islamist who had spent most of the 1980s facilitating an anti-Soviet jihad in Afghanistan. *The Satanic Verses* itself is less about the immigrant condition than about a helplessly Anglophilic Indian's profound ambivalence about a British ruling class that regards him as a wog.

Attacked for having defamed the Prophet, Rushdie withdrew from the terrain of history and politics he had previously staked, insisting that his novel was a 'work of art', and not reducible to an anti-Islam polemic. Upholding an exalted post-Christian notion of literature, he argued that the novel was the privileged realm of polyphony, doubt and argument. As such, it was naturally opposed and superior to the 'unarguable absolutes of religion' and incomprehensible to the Muslims protesting against his book – people prone to 'mass popular irrationalism'.

The world of unreformed Islam in this view presented a clear and present danger to the cherished beliefs, institutions and art forms of the secular and rational West. In his memoir, where Rushdie bizarrely decides to write about himself, or 'Joseph

Anton', his Conrad- and Chekhov-inspired alias, in the third person, he repeatedly points to his early intuitions and warnings about the atrocity suffered by the West on 9/11. 'He knew, as surely as he knew anything, that the fanatical cancer spreading through Muslim communities would in the end explode into the wider world beyond Islam.' Indeed, Rushdie's writings from this period anticipate many declarations of war on 'Islamofascism' after 9/11. As he wrote in 1990, defending *The Satanic Verses*,

'Battle lines are being drawn in India today,' one of my charac-
ters remarks. 'Secular versus religious, the light versus the dark.
Better you choose which side you are on.' Now that the battle
has spread to Britain, I only hope it will not be lost by default.
It is time for us to choose.

The ayatollah's cruelty and malice made many of Rushdie's choices for him. *Joseph Anton* conveys a clear and shaming picture of his ordeal – the soul-numbing humiliations of a subterranean existence, the scurrying from one safe house to another, and the endless negotiations with security staff for a few slivers of ordinary life. The reader is fully on Rushdie's side, and outraged when, in one of the book's few superbly rendered scenes, fear and confusion force him to re-embrace Islam before some Muslim scholars/busybodies.

There are fascinating details about Rushdie's parents in the memoir's early pages, which also appealingly evoke his years as a struggling writer with his first wife, Clarissa; few readers would fail, later in the book, to be moved by the account of her death and Rushdie's grief-tinged recall of his superseded self. Rushdie engagingly reveals the autobiographical energies that went into the making of such novels as *The Satanic Verses* and *Fury*. Anton's Herzog-style letters, addressed variously and randomly to famous people, critics and even God, effectively evoke the mind of an isolated and hunted man.

Yet the memoir, at 650 pages, often feels too long, overde-pendent on Rushdie's journals, and unquickened by hindsight, or its prose. Ostensibly deployed as a distancing device, the third-person narration frequently makes for awkward self-regard ('The clouds thickened over his head. But he found that his sentences could still form . . . his imagination still spark'). A peevish righteousness comes to pervade the memoir as Rushdie routinely and often repetitively censures those who criticised or disagreed with him. The long list of betrayers, carpers and timorous publishers includes Robert Gottlieb, Peter Mayer, John le Carré, Sonny Mehta, the *Independent* (evidently the 'house journal for British Islam'), Germaine Greer, John Berger and assorted policemen 'who believed he had done nothing of value in his life'. Small darts are also flung at James Wood, 'the malevolent Procrustes of literary criticism', Arundhati Roy, Joseph Brodsky, Louis de Bernières and many others.

Not just individuals, but entire countries, even races, are judged and frequently found wanting. The Danes lay on a battleship to protect Anton, who falls 'in love with the Nordic peoples because of their adherence to the highest principles of freedom'. 'America', we are told, 'had made it impossible for Britain to walk away from his defence.' Also, outside Britain, Anton 'was seen as likeable, funny, brave, talented and worthy of respect'.

There are some exceptions to British mean-mindedness. After one 'lovely evening' at Chequers, where the singer Mick Hucknall's 'hot girlfriend' is distractingly present, Anton confesses to a 'soft spot' for Tony Blair. 'You set out sincerely to change my life for the better,' he writes, and though this 'may not quite cancel out the invasion of Iraq', it does weigh in his 'personal scales'. Oddly, Anton seems to require no such moral balancing for the Sri Lankan strongman Mahinda Rajapaksa, who is commended for resisting Iranian pressure and green-lighting the filming of *Midnight's Children*; the responsibility of this authoritarian president and his brother in the massacre of tens of thousands of Tamil Hindus is passed over in silence. Nor does Anton record the piquant fact that the Hindu nationalists who noisily protested against the Indian decision to ban *The Satanic Verses* and, once in power, allowed him to visit India are implicated in the killings of thousands of Muslims in the previous two decades.

All this was also on the front pages into which, as Martin Amis famously remarked, Rushdie 'vanished' soon after the fatwa. However, *Joseph Anton* describes more accurately, if inadvertently, how Rushdie re-emerged, after the strangest ever writerly journey, in the gossip pages, aureoled by the wealth, power and glamour of the Western world.

Understandably, proximity to doting US senators in the 'heart of American power' would prove exhilarating for someone miserably on the run from a murderous regime; and it is one of the grotesque ironies of Rushdie's situation that freedom for him should become synonymous with a private plane with a 'Ralph Lauren interior' and a nine-car motorcade with motorcycle outriders. But the moral autonomy of literature, or the dignity of the individual artist, is not affirmed when a celebrated writer exults over being in the same 'mighty room' as Bernard-Henri Lévy and Nicolas Sarkozy.

A naive beguilement rather than sly irony frames Rushdie's accounts of hanging out with such very famous people as Jerry Seinfeld and Calista Flockhart. Madonna, narrowly missed at Tina Brown's immortal launch party for *Talk* magazine, is finally encountered at *Vanity Fair*'s Oscars bash in the company of Zadie Smith. At lunch at the Beverly Hills Hotel, Warren Beatty confesses that Padma Lakshmi, Rushdie's fourth wife, is so beautiful that it makes him 'want to faint'. And William Styron's genitalia are unexpectedly on display one convivial evening at Martha's Vineyard.

In this remembrance of parties and celebrities past, as in much of Rushdie's later fiction, eclecticism amounts to a disconcerting absence of discrimination – and tact. We learn uneasily of, among other infidelities, his wine-induced adultery with Jack Lang's 'beautiful and brilliant daughter'. His wives themselves are described much less flatteringly as gold-diggers or nags, squeezing Anton for more alimony or progeny. Cuttingly titled 'His Millenarian Illusion', the chapter about his marriage to Padma Lakshmi tries to show that his fourth wife's 'grand ambition and secret plans' for wealth and fame had 'nothing to do with the fulfilment of his deepest needs'.

A similar longing for self-affirmation fuels Rushdie's geopolitical analysis, where an obsession with the 'poison' of 'actually existing Islam' suppresses all nuance suggested by political and historical facts. He accuses Khomeini of taking 'his country into a useless war with its neighbours' and sees more evidence of Muslim irrationalism in the frenzied mourning provoked in Iran by the old fanatic's death. In fact, it was Saddam Hussein who invaded Iran, and then assaulted it with chemical weapons, with the consent, even support, of Western countries. This not only stoked a long-simmering anti-Westernism in Iran, which had been occupied by Russia and Britain during both world wars, and then suffered for decades the brutal dictatorship of the pro-American shah. The second-longest intra-nation war of the twentieth century, which killed nearly 1 million Iranians, also entrenched the Basij militia and Revolutionary Guards, made life harder for the moderates who cancelled Khomeini's fatwa and eventually helped bring Mahmoud Ahmadinejad to power.

One would respect Rushdie's wish to decline close scrutiny of a radioactive history and politics that have caused him so much distress. But he is too invested in his self-image as an unpopular 'Cassandra for his own time'. Back in 1989, he claims, 'nobody wanted to know what he knew' – that a 'self-exculpatory, paranoiac Islam is an ideology with widespread appeal' – and we didn't get this even after the terrorist attacks on 9/11, which, among other things, vindicated his critically ill-treated but evidently prophetic novel *Fury*.

'Of course this is "about Islam",' Rushdie quickly retorted in a *New York Times* op-ed to those who argued that 9/11 'isn't about Islam', or like Susan Sontag, a loyal friend and supporter, described the attacks as 'a consequence of specific American alliances and actions', such as the support of Saudi Arabia and fundamentalists in Afghanistan. According to him, 'the restoration of religion to the sphere of the personal, its depoliticisation, is the nettle that all Muslim societies must grasp in order to become modern.'

This French-style secularisation was and remains a tall order – even in the United States and much of Christian Europe. In the meantime, Rushdie seemed content to endorse the Anglo-American assault on Afghanistan, and, claiming that another 'war of liberation might just be one worth fighting', hailed the CIA-sponsored conman Ahmad Chalabi as 'the most likely first leader of a democratised Iraq'.

Joseph Anton, obscuring these stumbles, presents Rushdie as confidently in step with the march of history. 'The world of Islam', he reminds us he had written in 2001, 'must take on board the secularist-humanist principles on which the modern is based'; in 2011 'the young people of the Arab world' 'tried to transform their societies according to exactly these principles'.

Since Egyptians and Tunisians have subsequently elected Islamic parties to power, Rushdie has now changed his mind. Things have 'gone very wrong', he recently told Foreign Policy. 'One has to say that the Arab Spring is over.' Maybe, but long before Egypt and Tunisia, elected Islamic parties in the biggest Muslim country, Indonesia, supervised a transition from military despotism to electoral democracy.

In Iran itself a mass movement drawing on Islamic notions of justice and morality has ranged itself against Khomeini's discredited heirs. Fanatics and fundamentalists, non-Muslim as well as Muslim, remain a blight on many South Asian and Middle Eastern societies; sometimes, they violently disrupt public life in the West. But, arguably, it is the institutionalised procedures of torture, rendition, indefinite detention, extrajudicial execution through drones, secret trials and surveillance that have emerged in the West as the more serious threat to civil and human rights. The icon of free speech today is the Wikileaks source Chelsea Manning, fully exposed in her degrading confinement to the malevolence of an omnipotent intelligence and military establishment.

Meanwhile, cut-price white supremacists gunning down Sikhs, bombing mosques and burning the Qur'an, and the Nordic nationalist massacring multiculturalists and left-wingers have taken Rushdie's reform-minded diagnosis of a 'fanatical cancer' within Muslim communities to another level. 'Islam is a cancer, period,' according to the sinister California-based filmmaker whose calumnies about the Prophet provoke riots across the Muslim world. At the same time, Western states, after waging calamitously ill-conceived wars that killed and mutilated hundreds of thousands of Muslims, pursue a face-saving deal with people described by Rushdie as 'fascist, terrorist gangsters' – the Taliban.

Rushdie's neat oppositions between the secular and the religious, the light and the dark, and rational literary elites and irrational masses do not clarify the great disorder of the contemporary world. They belong to an intellectually simpler time, when non-Western societies, politically insignificant and little-known, could be judged solely by their success or failure in following the great example of the secular-humanist West; and writing literary fiction could seem enough to make one feel, as Tim Parks wrote in a review of Rushdie's novel *The Ground beneath Her Feet*, 'engaged on the right side of some global moral and political battle'.

Indeed, such complacencies of imperial intellectual cultures were what Rushdie had bravely attacked in his brilliant early phase. 'Works of art, even works of entertainment,' he had pointed out in 1984, 'do not come into being in a social and political vacuum; and . . . the way they operate in a society cannot be separated from politics, from history. For every text, a context.' No text in our time has had contexts more various and illuminating than *The Satanic Verses*, or mixed politics and literature more inextricably, and with deeper consequences for so many. In *Joseph Anton*, however, Rushdie continues to reveal an unwillingness or inability to grasp them, or to abandon the conceit, useful in fiction but misleading outside it, that the personal is the geopolitical.

2012

5

The Man of Fourteen Points

*On Woodrow Wilson and the Birth
of Liberal Internationalism*

Early in *The Wilsonian Moment*, Erez Manela tells a story about Ho Chi Minh that I often heard in student communist circles in India. Ho was an indigent worker in Paris when Woodrow Wilson arrived in the city in 1919 with a plan to make the world 'safe for democracy'. Inspired by Wilson's advocacy of national self-determination, Ho sought an audience with the US president, hoping to persuade him to use his new influence to restore Vietnamese rule in French Indo-China. He carefully quoted from the US Declaration of Independence in his petition. In Manela's more poignant version, he also rented a morning suit. Needless to say, Ho got nowhere near Wilson or any other Western leader; he found a sympathetic audience only among French communists.

Many communist students I knew in India repeated with reverence the story of Ho's failed mission because it appeared to confirm their urtext, Lenin's *Imperialism: The Highest Stage of Capitalism*. Written in 1916, this pamphlet had proved that Wilson was as unlikely to restore Indo-China to the Vietnamese as he was to withdraw American troops from Panama. The United States was as much an imperialist power as Britain and Japan, greedy for resources, territory and markets, part of a capitalist world system of oppression and plunder whose inherent instability had caused the Great War.

Lenin's text came to many of us in the Indian provinces as an exhilarating revelation. No amount of praise appeared sufficient for the Soviet leader who had pre-empted Wilson in calling for national self-determination. Hadn't he exposed the secret agreement between France, Britain and tsarist Russia to carve up the Middle East, among other booty of the imperialist war? True to his anti-imperialist rhetoric, he had promised autonomy to Russia's ethnic minorities and had voluntarily given up the special concessions Russia enjoyed in subjugated China along with other Western powers and Japan.

Communist study circles did not, of course, discuss what Stalin made of Lenin's promise to Russia's ethnic nationalities, or how Asian communists overturned Lenin's facile equation – imperialism equals monopoly capitalism – when in the early 1960s China accused the Soviet Union of imperialist aggression. I learned even less about the capitalist rival of Marxist internationalism: liberal internationalism, which originated in the Progressive Movement of the United States and, as eloquently articulated by Woodrow Wilson, enjoyed worldwide appeal for a few hopeful months after the end of the First World War, when a new world order seemed likely to rise on the ruins of the Austro-Hungarian, German, Ottoman and Russian Empires.

Trawling through four national archives, Manela has produced an immensely rich and important work of comparative politics centred on the 'Wilsonian moment', which he dates from autumn 1918 to spring 1919. 'Disseminated to a growing global audience', Wilson's rousing speeches leading up to the Paris Peace Conference earned him, as Maynard Keynes later recorded, 'a prestige and a moral influence throughout the world unequalled in history'. Emboldened by him, nationalist leaders in Egypt and India joined Sinn Féin in seriously challenging British authority, and China and Korea grew more aggressive in their demands for political and economic autonomy.

Anti-colonialists everywhere had been transfixed by the swift rise of the United States, a new political and economic power rare among Western nations for possessing a strong tradition of anti-imperialism. For much of the nineteenth century, the United States had been isolationist in its foreign policy and protectionist in its economic; and its footprint was light in Asia and Africa, where, as even Raymond Aron conceded, the natives did not need to read or even understand Lenin, or have to deal with a repressive imperial police state, to identify Europe with imperialism. There was enough evidence for it in everyday life and memory: 'the exploitation of raw materials without any attempt to create local industry; the destruction of native crafts and the stunted growth of industrial development that resulted from the influx of European goods; high interest rates on loans; ownership of major businesses by foreign capitalists'.

The war, which enfeebled the economies of the major imperialist powers – Britain, Germany and France – and further discredited their regimes, endowed America with both power and moral prestige. Wilson, who barely had a foreign policy before war broke out in Europe in 1914, wasn't slow to realise the implications of European turmoil for the United States; and he fleshed out a new and noble American sense of mission before he reluctantly took his country into the European war. 'We are provincials no longer,' he famously declared in his second inaugural address in March 1917. Though still publicly opposed to American intervention in the war, he insisted that 'our own fortunes as a nation are involved whether we would have it so or not.'

In speeches addressed to 'the peoples of the countries now at war' he burnished his credentials as a mediator who could negotiate what he called (borrowing the phrase from Walter Lippmann, the energetic young editor of the *New Republic*) a 'peace without victory'. Later, he would propose a much more unusual and high-minded plan for enduring peace – replacing militarist regimes with democracies – which liberal intellectuals as well as conservative politicians would invoke with diminishing returns throughout the twentieth century, culminating in the invasion of Iraq in 2003, which inspired the *New Republic* to declare George W. Bush 'the most Wilsonian president since Wilson himself'.

Wilson had begun to outline the American preference for regime change in unfriendly countries well before he declared war on Germany. Faced in late 1913 with revolution and the likely rejection of American influence in Mexico, he had decided to 'teach the South American republics to elect good men'. 'When properly directed,' he claimed, 'there is no people not fitted for self-government.' Wilson was also convinced that proper direction in the post-war order could be provided only by the United States. When his peace overtures failed, he went to war in April 1917, still confident that 'we are chosen, and prominently chosen, to show the way to the nations of the world how they shall walk in the paths of liberty.'

Wilson, an academic by training, was fortified in his convictions by such liberal intellectuals as John Dewey, Walter Lippmann and Herbert Croly (co-founder of the *New Republic*), who believed that by joining the war America would make the world safe for democracy rather than, as was the case, help the Allied powers deliver a knockout blow to the Germans. As Randolph Bourne, a young critic whose opposition to American intervention made him an outcast among liberal intellectuals, pointed out as early as August 1917, the United States lost whatever leverage it had had as an impartial mediator when it declared war on Germany.

Nevertheless, Wilson pressed ahead with his scheme for a democratic international order, which he hoped would be cemented by a League of Nations. Speaking to Congress in January 1918 he revealed his most ambitious project yet: a fourteen-point manifesto for the new world envisaged by the United States. Secret diplomacy was to have no place, and free trade, popular government, freedom of the seas, the reduction of armaments, the rights of small countries, and an association of nations to keep the peace were to be the new articles of faith.

Wilson's Fourteen Points would have been lofty ideals at any time (God, as Clemenceau joked, had only ten). They were particularly unrealistic during a global war that would soon end with Britain, France and Japan adding to their possessions in the Middle East, Africa and East Asia. As it turned out, Wilson was soon forced to compromise his ideals while dealing with the victorious allies at the post-war peace conference in Paris.

It is likely that Wilson would not have upped the rhetorical ante in January 1918 if the Bolsheviks had not withdrawn Russia from the war and called on workers and soldiers to cease fighting one another and become revolutionaries against their own rulers. In asserting that America was fighting for a better world, Wilson was trying to undercut Bolshevik claims that the war was a struggle among imperialist powers, with the victorious elites likely to share the spoils. He aimed to influence those Americans and Europeans who, growing tired of the endless fighting, appeared dangerously susceptible to Bolshevik propaganda. Almost by accident, he reached a much bigger and more receptive audience in the colonised world.

Marxism was then being studied and debated in many Asian cities and towns where European traders and missionaries had set up Western-style educational institutions. But the Russian Revolution and its anti-imperialist ethos was not much known. The United States, too, was an unknown player in international relations, and its record in the Philippines and Latin America – Wilson's imposition, for instance, of military protectorates in Haiti and Nicaragua – went mostly unexamined. Boosted by a slick propaganda campaign, Wilson easily won the first round of his war of ideas with the Bolsheviks, heralding a world where small nations would enjoy the right of self-determination. And so 'when peace came,' Manela writes, 'colonial peoples moved to claim their place in that world on the basis of Wilson's proclamations.'

In Egypt, Sa'd Zaghlul, a liberal reformist, organised a new political party called the Wafd ('delegation') in preparation for the Paris Peace Conference. Soon after war began, the British had declared Egypt a protectorate of the British Empire, formalising their invasion and occupation of the country in 1882. Zaghlul, who is known in Egypt as the Father of the Nation, denounced the protectorate as illegal and hoped to enlist Wilson on his side. 'No people more than the Egyptian people', he wrote in a telegram to Wilson, 'has felt strongly the joyous emotion of the birth of a new era which, thanks to your virile action, is soon going to impose itself upon the universe.'

Inspired by Wilson's rhetoric, nationalist leaders in Korea wrote their own Declaration of Independence. Expectations ran even higher in India and China, which had contributed more than a million soldiers and labourers to the Allied war effort in Europe and the Middle East. Tagore wanted to dedicate one of his books to Wilson and, stirred by Wilson's wartime speeches, Hindu and Muslim leaders of the Indian National Congress jointly demanded to send their delegates – Gandhi among them – to represent India at the peace conference. In Beijing students gathered in front of the American Embassy chanting, 'Long live President Wilson!' Liang Qichao, the reformist intellectual and earliest inspiration of Mao Zedong, went to Paris to ensure that China's sovereignty was respected by the victorious powers, particularly Japan, which, in a campaign green-lighted by Britain during the war, had seized German-held territory in the Shandong Peninsula.

Asians and Africans accustomed to stonewalling colonial officials were naturally attracted to the generous promises of the American president. But Wilson, a southerner who shared the reflexive racism of many in his class and generation (and liked to tell jokes about 'darkies'), was an unlikely hero in the alleys of Delhi, Cairo and Canton. Piously Presbyterian, and a helpless Anglophile (he had courted his wife with quotations from Bagehot and Burke), he had hoped that in the Philippines and Puerto Rico the United States would follow the British tradition of instructing 'less civilised' peoples in law and order.

After all, 'they are children and we are men in these deep matters of government and justice.'

Ho Chi Minh would not have bothered to rent a morning suit had he known that Wilson believed as much as his bellicose rival Theodore Roosevelt in America's responsibility to shoulder the white man's burden. In January 1917, Wilson argued that America should stay out of the war in order, as he said in a Cabinet meeting, to 'keep the white race strong against the yellow – Japan for instance'. He believed, as he told his secretary of state Robert Lansing, that '"white civilisation" and its domination over the world rested largely on our ability to keep this country intact.' Though apparently all-encompassing, his rhetoric about self-determination was aimed at the European peoples – Poles, Romanians, Czechs, Serbs – who were part of the German, Austro-Hungarian and Ottoman Empires. In his effort to establish the League of Nations as a framework for collective security and enduring peace in Europe, he had little interest in persuading Britain and France to relinquish their colonial possessions.

Not that this was possible. Wilson had had his chance in the spring of 1917 when he first heard of the secret treaties that outlined how Britain, France, Japan and Italy planned to divide up entire empires among themselves after the war. He could have made American intervention contingent on the Allied powers cancelling these arrangements. Instead, he pretended that the treaties didn't exist, and even tried to prevent their publication in the US after the Bolsheviks exposed their existence.

Travelling to Europe in 1919, Wilson hoped to appeal directly to the people, over the heads of their leaders. Ecstatic crowds in France and Italy credited him with hastening the end of a deeply unloved war, but in Paris he confronted hardened and cynical imperialists in Lloyd George and Clemenceau. After several internecine wars, Europe's imperial powers had arrived at a balance-of-power politics. Their representatives in Paris hoped to restore the equilibrium that war had disrupted by reducing Germany's power; and Wilson kept compromising in the hope that old and new problems in the world order would be solved by his cherished League of Nations.

Mao Zedong caught Wilson's haplessness in Paris perfectly:

> Wilson in Paris was like an ant on a hot skillet. He didn't know what to do. He was surrounded by thieves like Clemenceau, Lloyd George, Makino and Orlando. He heard nothing except accounts of receiving certain amounts of territory and of reparations worth so much in gold. He did nothing except to attend various kinds of meetings where he could not speak his mind. One day a Reuters telegram read: 'President Wilson has finally agreed with Clemenceau's view that Germany not be admitted to the League of Nations.' When I saw the words 'finally agreed', I felt sorry for him for a long time. Poor Wilson!

The League, rejected by the US Senate, turned out to be a fiasco. Wilson's failures in Paris angered and eventually lost him his liberal supporters at the *New Republic*. Defeated over Germany, he barely put up a fight when it came to the rights of non-European peoples, many of whom – including the Persians and Syrians – did not get a hearing at the conference. Though backed by a majority of votes, a clause for racial equality proposed by the Japanese delegation foundered because Wilson feared alienating the British and their Australian allies, who wanted to maintain their White Australia policy.

To a large extent Anglophilia blinded Wilson and his advisers, mostly members of the East Coast WASP elite, to anti-colonial feelings in Asia and Africa. The American secretary of state fully backed British rule over Egypt. Allen Dulles, a future Cold Warrior who was then a State Department official, suggested that Egyptian demands 'should not even be acknowledged'. The British, working the special relationship to their advantage, ensured that petitions sent to Wilson in Paris were filed away never to be heard of again; they also told Wilson that Tagore was a dangerous revolutionary (he didn't get permission for his dedication).

Indian and Korean nationalists didn't get anywhere near Paris. India was represented by a delegation picked by the British, including a maharajah in a flamboyant red turban. The Egyptians suffered a deeper humiliation. In March 1919, the British arrested Zaghlul and deported him to Malta, provoking widespread public protests in Egypt – what later came to be known as the 1919 Revolution. Faced with nationwide revolt, the British relented and allowed Zaghlul to go to Paris. But while he was honing his English, the British managed to persuade the Americans that Bolsheviks had plotted with Islamic fanatics to fuel the unrest in Egypt. Zaghlul was on his way from Marseille to Paris when Wilson recognised the British protectorate. The Egyptian journalist Muhammad Haykal expressed the general outrage when he wrote,

> Here was the man of the Fourteen Points, among them the right to self-determination, denying the Egyptian people its right to self-determination . . . And doing all that before the delegation on behalf of the Egyptian people had arrived in Paris to defend its claim, and before President Wilson had heard one word from them! Is this not the ugliest of treacheries?!

The sense of betrayal was even stronger among millions of Chinese who, unlike the Indians and the Koreans, were adequately represented at the conference. Wilson was sympathetic to Chinese claims on Japanese-occupied Shandong, but he could not persuade Lloyd George and Clemenceau to rescind their wartime promises to Japan. News of China's failure in May 1919 brought enraged students out on the streets of Beijing, denouncing the US president as a liar. Demonstrations and strikes erupted across China in what would later be known as the May Fourth Movement, an explosion of intellectual and political energy that reverberated through the next decades.

'The emergence of the Wilsonian moment had heralded the end of a great conflict, the European war,' Manela writes, 'but its dissipation gave rise to a greater one still, one "between East and West, between imperialism and self-determination".' Western powers could not forever ignore or suppress the nationalist claims, and in 1922 China, which had refused to sign the Treaty of Versailles, received a new settlement, restoring Japanese-held areas in Shandong to its sovereignty. Egypt remained volatile, and in the same year the British were forced to grant it a degree of self-rule. In India they tried to retain the repressive policies introduced during the war; but the killing of 400 demonstrators in Amritsar in April 1919 only accelerated the transformation of the Indian National Congress from a gentleman's debating club into a mass political party.

'The new era of self-determination', as Manela writes, had come, but 'it was one of conflict rather than co-operation.' Wilson's apparent complicity with old-style imperialists united many educated Asians in what Manela calls 'cynical hostility to Western civilisation'. The early generation of Asian intellectuals and activists had looked to their Western conquerors with awe and admiration. Their nationalism tended to be frankly 'derivative', an admission that those who wanted to catch up with the West could do no better than learn from its industrialism and the obviously superior institutions of liberal democracy. But such bourgeois gradualism no longer seemed so attractive to many anti-colonial intellectuals after the Paris Peace Conference.

Liberals such as Tagore who believed in synthesis, a dialogue between West and East, felt particularly humiliated. Gandhi had never expected much of Woodrow Wilson but Tagore had, and on a lecture tour of the United States in 1930 he unexpectedly turned on his American audience, who were probably expecting to be educated about Eastern spirituality. 'Our appeal does not reach you,' Tagore said, 'because you respond only to the appeal of power. Japan appealed to you and you answered because she was able to prove she would make herself as obnoxious as you can.' Only a deep lingering bitterness could have made the poet tell a New York audience including Franklin Roosevelt, Henry Morgenthau and Sinclair Lewis that 'a great portion of the world suffers from your civilisation'.

Travelling to Paris, Wilson may have believed that liberalism 'must be more liberal than ever before, it must even be radical, if civilisation is to escape the typhoon'. But secular liberalism in Muslim countries under direct British control had been tainted well before the true scale of British duplicity in the Middle East was revealed at the end of the war. Even the moderate Islamic scholar, Egypt's grand mufti, Muhammad Abduh said that 'we Egyptians . . . believed once in English liberalism and English sympathy; but we believe no longer, for facts are stronger than words. Your liberalness we see plainly is only for yourselves, and your sympathy with us is that of the wolf for the lamb which he designs to eat.'

In China, hostility to Japan and anger at the country's own fractious warlords fused with anti-Western sentiment to create a sharper-edged nationalism. Western-style liberalism would continue to enjoy a vogue among educated, well-travelled Chinese. But the 20-year-old poet Qu Qiubai, a student of Buddhism who later became a crucial contact in Moscow for the fledgling Chinese Communist Party, found – and he was not alone – that 'the sharp pain of imperialistic oppression' liberated him from the illusions of 'impractical democratic reforms'. Mao Zedong was left with an enduring suspicion of Western motives and policies, and a broader awareness of the political possibilities available to subjugated peoples. As Manela puts it,

> The Chinese protest against international injustice, Mao discovered, was part of a wider pattern of uprisings of marginalised groups in international society striving for the recognition of their rights to self-determination and equality. Only the transformation of the norms and practices of international relations would allow China to attain its rightful place among nations.

Manela believes that 'the rise of Communism in China and elsewhere in the early 1920s was part of that quest, as the failure of the liberal anti-colonialism of the Wilsonian moment to fulfil its promise sparked a search for alternative ideologies.' After initial successes, Wilson's influence was overtaken by Lenin's; China may have been 'lost' to communism not, as the Cold Warriors alleged, in 1949, but in 1919. State-regulated capitalism rather than central planning would bring China – and India – close to their rightful place among nations in the age of globalisation; but the change of economic models did not diminish the lustre of national sovereignty. Nationalist feeling, defined by these early anti-imperialist campaigns for equality, remains potent in both countries, continuing to fuel middle-class Chinese and Indian desires for greater dignity in a world where economic power is shifting back to Asia.

Faced with an enormous task of compression, Manela can only outline how anti-colonial nationalism drew on a great suspicion of Western politicians with noble ideals as well as of those with guns. It would be too much to expect him also to examine Wilson's legacy, the 'liberal internationalism' whose tattered flag was held up most recently by liberal hawks supporting the invasion of Iraq. It is hard, however, to read his book without wondering how those espousing compassionately liberal policies at home become susceptible to violent humanitarianism abroad – what Randolph Bourne incredulously called 'war in the interests of democracy'. 'This was almost the sum of their philosophy,' Bourne wrote of his old friends. 'The primitive idea to which they regressed became almost insensibly translated into a craving for action.'

Wilson chose to cast American interests abroad in highly moral, even mystical, terms, claiming that, as Bourne described it, the United States had been 'ordained as a nation to lead all erring brothers towards the light of liberty and democracy'; and since the objectives of liberal democracies coincide, Germany could become peaceful by discarding its militarist regime and embracing democracy with American help. (The more corporate-friendly version of this peculiarly American idea is Thomas Friedman's belief that countries where McDonald's burgers are eaten never go to war with each other.)

In Paris, Lloyd George and Clemenceau demonstrated that leaders of democracies could be just as brazenly imperialistic as military dictators. But then Wilson, who had presided over a serious erosion of civil liberties at home during the war, was no stranger to moral compromises in foreign policy: he had supported, for instance, China's militarist president Yuan Shikai against the nationalists allied with Sun Yat-sen in 1913 in the hope of keeping America's 'Open Door' to China.

Such expediencies were later to define the Cold War, in which the United States, as Dean Acheson unironically proclaimed, was 'willing to help people who believe the way we do, to continue to live the way they want to live'. Or, as the current national security adviser, trying to explain Bush's recent farewell calls on pro-American dictators in the Middle East, put it, 'These folks . . . are on board with the freedom agenda and they are pursuing it in their own fashion.'

Wilson's rhetorical achievement – which distinguished him sharply from traditional European practitioners of realpolitik – was to present America's strategic and political interests as moral imperatives, and its foreign interventions as necessary acts of international responsibility. European leaders periodically stressed their civilising mission, but no one before Wilson endowed national exceptionalism with such a modern and unimpeachably noble aspiration as 'democracy'.

Intoxicated by the moral passions of Wilsonianism, American liberal intellectuals would work harder than their European counterparts to justify wars that political leaders promised would make the world safe for democracy. These sincere believers would also be more vulnerable, when faced with the collapse of their bold schemes, to the guilt-laden 'fear that what we had meant, and what alone could justify it all, was *not* the meaning and the justification of those who will decide' – Lippmann's words, which handily summarise the long, tormented mea culpas produced by liberal hawks after the catastrophe in Iraq.

What neither hard-headed politicians nor their intellectual dupes fully understood was how the rhetoric of liberalism and democracy had gone down in the colonised world. Certainly Wilson, working deep in a world run by and for white men, could have little sense of the bitterness and disillusionment felt by his 'darkie' admirers. But the excuse of racial and intellectual seclusion could not be claimed by apparently liberal politicians and journalists who stridently echoed Wilson's rhetoric after the collapse of communism when the world seemed riper for remaking, more ready to absorb Western values while fulfilling Western interests, than at any time since 1919.

'We are all internationalists now,' Tony Blair declared to the Chicago Economic Club in April 1999, in the midst of bombing Serbia. 'In the end,' he said, 'values and interests merge. If we can establish and spread the values of liberty, the rule of law, human rights and an open society then that is in our national interests too.' Dazzled by the wealth and power of *fin de siècle* America (as though returning the compliment after decades of Anglophilia among the American ruling class), Blair and other New Labourites turned out to be the most eager European consumers of Wilson's potpourri of values and interests. Their eloquence proved useful to the most Wilsonian – but also the most inarticulate – of American presidents, and his cronies.

The victories of the Cold War – and the giddy speculation that history had reached the ideological terminus of liberal democracy – revived illusions of omnipotence among an Anglo-American political and media elite that has always known very little about the modern world it claims to have made. Consequently, almost every event since the end of the Cold War – the rise of radical Islam, of India and China; the assertiveness of oil-rich Russia, Iran and Venezuela – has come as a shock, a rude reminder that the natives of Delhi, Cairo and Beijing have geopolitical ambitions of their own, not to mention a sense of history marked by resentment and suspicion of the metropolitan West. The liberal internationalists persist, trying to revive the Wilsonian moment in places where Anglo-American liberalism has been seen as an especially aggressive form of hypocrisy. Increasingly, however, they expose themselves as the new provincials, dangerously blundering about in a volatile world.

2008

6

Bland Fanatics

On Liberalism and Colonialism

Visiting Africa and Asia in the 1960s, Conor Cruise O'Brien discovered that many people in former colonies were 'sickened by the word "liberalism"'. They saw it as an 'ingratiating moral mask which a toughly acquisitive society wears before the world it robs'. O'Brien – 'incurably liberal' himself (at least in this early phase of his career) – was dismayed. He couldn't understand why liberalism had come to be seen as an 'ideology of the rich, the elevation into universal values of the codes which favoured the emergence, and favour the continuance, of capitalist society'. This seemed to him too harsh a verdict on a set of ideas and dispositions that appeared to promote democratic government, constitutionalism, the rule of law, a minimal state, property rights, self-regulating markets and the empowerment of the autonomous rational individual.

Liberal ideas in the West had emerged in a variety of political and economic settings, in both Europe and North America. They originated in the Reformation's stress on individual responsibility, and were shaped to fit the mould of the market freedoms that capitalism would need if it was to thrive (the right to private property and free labour, freedom from state regulation and taxation). They did not seem particularly liberal to the peoples subjugated by British, French and American imperialism in the eighteenth and nineteenth centuries. Contradictions and elisions haunted the rhetoric of liberalism from the beginning. 'How is it', Samuel Johnson asked about secession-minded American colonists, 'that we hear the loudest yelps for liberty among the drivers of negroes?' John Stuart Mill credited India's free-trading British overlords with benign liberal intentions towards a people self-evidently incapable of self-rule. 'Despotism', he wrote, 'is a legitimate mode of government in dealing with barbarians, provided the end be their improvement.' Alexis de Tocqueville, by contrast, felt no need of the ingratiating moral mask; the French colonial project in Algeria was a glorious enterprise, a vital part of French nation building after decades of political turmoil.

It wasn't only the entwined history of liberalism and imperialism that in the 1960s made many Asians and Africans suspect American and European liberals of being 'false friends'. As O'Brien admitted, during the Cold War many Western liberals – such as those who were against imposing sanctions on South Africa – upheld the most illiberal forms of anti-communism. Theorists who promoted free enterprise and equal rights as a formula for prosperity that all new nations could adopt often came from countries with long histories of economic protectionism and institutionalised racism. The new post-colonial nations had their own alternatives to Western liberalism. Even non-communist countries such as India and South Korea put in place systems of government based on a mixture of central planning and market intervention. Raymond Aron, worrying about the appeal of communism in Asia in the 1950s, suggested that non-liberal policies and institutions appealed to many state builders in Asia because it was clear to them that liberal methods in politics and economics were doomed to fail.

The collapse of communist regimes in 1989 emboldened the 'bland fanatics of Western civilisation', as the resolutely anti-communist Reinhold Niebuhr called them, 'who regard the highly contingent achievements of our culture as the final form and norm of human existence'. It wasn't too difficult for Cold War liberalism, defined and deformed by its ideological battle with communism, to reincarnate itself as neo-liberalism. More than one influential Western commentator in the 1990s and early 2000s outlined the new institutional framework within which latecomers to the modern world, without the benefits of slave ownership and colonialism, could achieve the virtues of individual liberty. Thomas Friedman's recommendations to the world's stragglers included the 'values of hard work, thrift, honesty, patience and tenacity', as well as 'export-oriented free market strategies based on privatisation of state companies, deregulation of financial markets, currency adjustments, foreign direct investment, shrinking subsidies, lowering protectionist tariff barriers, and introduction of more flexible labour laws'. The financial crisis of 2008 redirected Friedman's attention to the manifold problems of rising inequality, debt and the shrinking middle class in the US. Liberalism is deeply implicated in the crisis, as the path to it was laid by free-market ideologues who demanded more liberty and less regulation from the state as elected politicians removed all restraints on corporate greed. Unlike Edmund Fawcett, a former *Economist* journalist who seems aware of its crisis of credibility, Alan Ryan and Larry Siedentop continue to uphold liberalism as a universal ideology to which all political progress has been leading. 'The only morally acceptable form of democracy', Ryan writes, is 'liberal democracy', and liberalism gives 'the ordinary person a degree of intellectual, spiritual and occupational freedom the ancient world never dreamed of'. Siedentop is convinced that 'we in the West' must 'shape the conversation of mankind', but that we must first understand 'the moral depth of our own tradition'.

The suspicion that Ryan and Siedentop are working with anachronistic assumptions – derived from a sanguine nineteenth-century philosophy of history and progress – is deepened by their failure even to mention the current challengers in the West to liberalism and liberal democracy: the racist Republican right in America and quasi-fascist movements across Western Europe. The political landscape elsewhere, from Xi Jinping's China to

Evo Morales's Bolivia, from Islamic State in Syria and Iraq to Thailand's monarchy-backed military despotism, features a variety of political forms, social movements and political mobilisations, and looks further from Western liberalism than ever. Representative democracy and global capitalism were supposed to work hand in hand to usher barbarian peoples into a future of prosperity and stability, but have turned out to be deeply antagonistic to each other even in India, which Western liberal democrats had long cherished as their most diligent apprentice in the East.

A universal bellicosity confirms Santayana's suspicion that 'liberalism has merely cleared a field in which every soul and every corporate interest may fight with every other for domination.' Siedentop acknowledges this reality only in his assertion that 'we are in a competition of beliefs' with Chinese-style capitalism and Islam, which 'offends some of our deepest intuitions'. This is 'a strange and disturbing moment in Western history', but only because Europeans 'have lost touch with their own moral intuitions'. Americans understand that 'liberal thought is the offspring of Christianity', but Europeans don't, with potentially ruinous consequences: Muslims, for instance, are 'frequently encouraged to look forward to replacing the laws of the nation state with sharia "law"', when secularism, 'Europe's noblest achievement', 'should be its primary contribution to the creation of a world order'.

In *Democracy in Europe*, Siedentop endorsed pluralism – 'a competition of values and institutions' – as 'the defining characteristic of European civilisation', and proposed, optimistically, the creation of a European super-state on the federal model of the United States. The European Union is now unravelling politically and economically, and Siedentop appears to seek comfort in the identity politics of the elite – based on the hoary notion of a West shaped by Christianity – that even such guardians of *laïcité* as Nicolas Sarkozy have expediently embraced. Inconvenient facts such as the growth of Christian fundamentalism in America can be explained away as a 'reaction to the threat of radical Islam'.

Convinced that 'moral beliefs' have given a clear overall 'direction' to Western history, Siedentop mentions capitalism only once in *Inventing the Individual*, while critics of the liberal tradition in the West – including Marx, Burckhardt, Nietzsche and Carl Schmitt – are almost completely ignored. Ryan and Fawcett offer a more capacious account of liberalism, but are just as indifferent to mankind's many other conversations with itself, especially those held outside the West. 'Political thought as we understand it began in Athens,' Ryan asserts in the serenely pedagogical 'Great Books' style of the early twentieth century; the hundreds of pages of lucid exposition that follow show no awareness of Chanakya, Mencius, Ashoka or al-Ghazali, or of traditions of political thought older than Greece's. Ryan mentions Islamic philosophy only to traduce it by dwelling on such fundamentalist agitators as Sayyid Qutb, whose shrill anti-Westernism became, after 9/11, the lens through which self-styled defenders of the liberal-democratic West like Martin Amis chose to view Islam. In this version of Western liberalism, it seems enough to posit the defence of individual liberty as the highest task of politics, and then dismiss all other political traditions as illiberal, or even fanatical.

A less emollient history of Western liberalism emerges from recent scholarship on nineteenth- and early twentieth-century Asia, where liberal ideas originating in the West were resisted, appropriated, interpreted and transformed. In Asia, notions of the autonomous individual, minimal government and the invisible hand of the market did not grow out of the Reformation or the needs of an expansionist capitalism. In India, China and Japan, the state or the national community – rather than self-motivated individuals – were expected to generate political, economic and social transformation. In the wake of Western imperialism, these societies felt obliged to replicate every process and institution that appeared to have made the West omnipotent and wealthy: secularisation; nationalism or a sense of national identity; a centralised bureaucracy and an army capable of protecting society from internal and external security challenges; a division of labour between political, social and economic realms; and popular participation in politics. But catching up with the West seemed impossible without a strong state. Liberalism seemed attractive largely because it promised to advance the urgent project of state-led modernisation.

Colonialism, and the Western-style pedagogy it introduced, did expose a large number of educated people in Asia to the post-Enlightenment bourgeois notions of individual freedom and autonomy. The growing self-consciousness of this elite helped create Asia's modern art, literature and philosophy, and individualist ideas sparked a quest – in colonial Calcutta as much as in Meiji Tokyo – to redefine the self and its relation to the collective and the state. But liberal individualism that did not stress the role of community and society in the formation of the moral self was generally not acceptable. 'The valuation of the liberal individual in India', the late Christopher Bayly wrote in *Recovering Liberties: Indian Thought in the Age of Liberalism and Empire*, was 'impregnated with the idea of sharing, generosity and compassion . . . dramatised by tropes from the Indian classics, the Vedanta and particularly the *Bhagavad Gita*'.

Bal Gangadhar Tilak was the clearest exponent of this view, building on an already strong critique of Western liberalism that had emerged in Bengal. By the late nineteenth century, India's British rulers had replaced violent appropriation and plunder by more subtle forms of oppression and control. Heavy taxation and export policies were introduced as part of the imperial bonanza of secure property rights and the rule of law that had replaced arbitrary oriental despotism. Many Bengali readers of Mill shared his conviction that British rule offered Indians the most reliable path to civilisation and modernity. Others took a dimmer view of the acquisitive Westerners. In Tilak's assessment, both self-interest and the utilitarian principle of 'the greatest good for the greatest number' belonged to a crassly materialist conception of the world, and offered no guide to ethical action, let alone happiness or contentment. He defined individual liberty in otherworldly terms, positing *moksha*, liberation from material attachments, as life's ultimate goal. Liberalism in this version was a system of duties and obligations: ethical conduct, not rational self-interest, came first.

In promulgating an idea of moral freedom and individual rights that had little to do with Mill's conception of progress, Gandhi, too, proposed a new idea of political selfhood. True civilisation (or *Sudharo*), he wrote in *Hind Swaraj*, is 'that mode of conduct by which man does his duty. Performance of duty is the observance of morality. To observe morality is to discipline our mind and our senses.' Many other members of an upper-caste Hindu elite upheld a superior ideal of personal and national culture against the utilitarian obsessions of British imperialists and the commercialism of a rising Indian capitalist bourgeoisie. There could be no easy transition from their ideal of self-purification to 'possessive individualism' of the European kind. In any case, as Bayly points out, any such transition would be constrained by 'the weight of Hindu and Muslim tradition, Indian familial and caste relations, the self-abnegating interpretation of Hindu devotionalism and the colonial context more broadly'. Even sympathetic readers of Mill, proto-liberals such as M.G. Ranade, Gopal Krishna Gokhale and Dadabhai Naoroji, were pushed by the unavoidable facts of deindustrialisation and widespread impoverishment into economic nationalism by the end of the nineteenth century. Horrific famines were caused by a fanatical British allegiance to free trade; the great suffering, which the colonial government did little or nothing to alleviate, rendered impossible an Indian liberal argument against government interventions in the market.

Indeed, free trade, accompanied as it was by brute coercion, never had much of a chance in Asia, where the most influential Western economist was Friedrich List, not Adam Smith. List had rejected Smith's free-trade theory as unsuitable for nineteenth-century conditions of rivalry and inequality between nation states. List had also spotted that laissez-faire economies favoured the trading interests of Britain, which had industrialised before everyone else. Economic nationalism seemed imperative to Asian countries entering – very late in the game – the race to indus-trial modernity. The Indian mutation of classical liberalism was from the beginning more communitarian, Bayly wrote, 'more concerned with the fate of society rather than the individual, and more hospitable to the idea of state intervention in the economy'.

The same is true of the reception of liberalism in China, where foreign invasions and civil war meant it was even less likely to be embodied in national institutions. Chinese thinkers such as Liang Qichao and Yan Fu grappled with abstract European notions of the rights-bearing individual against a background of China's semi-colonisation by Western powers, encroachments on its territory by a rapidly modernising Japan, the crumbling of the old monarchical system with its notion of universal king-ship, and the exigencies of nationalism and state building. As with Tilak and Gandhi's efforts in India, there were attempts to redefine the self in terms of duties and responsibilities, and to propose new models of social and political community. Laissez-faire was judged incompatible with the Chinese com-munitarian tradition. And the meaning of the Western liberal concepts adopted by Chinese intellectuals via Meiji Japan was shaped by the cultural assumptions embedded in their language. The Japanese term *jiyu*, which was derived from the Chinese word *ziyou*, was the standard translation of 'liberty'. But the loanword could not be cleansed of the implication of selfish-ness carried by the Chinese term. 'Laissez-faire' became *ziyou fangren* in Chinese, which also connotes rejection of responsi-bility for one's behaviour. Yan Fu (1854–1921), who translated the works of Adam Smith, John Stuart Mill, Thomas Huxley and Herbert Spencer, had trouble with such terms as 'privacy', 'taste', 'rights' and 'legitimate self-interest'; he also struggled with 'will', 'reason', 'judgement' and 'individual spontaneity'. Yan believed that the West had mastered the art of channelling individual energy into national strength, and was convinced that only a free society and democratic institutions could guarantee a similar outcome for China, but even so he could not break with the Confucian ideal of a non-competitive world in which self-interest is subordinated to social harmony. His 'liberalism' did not conceive of individual rights as an end in themselves; rather, in his utilitarian calculation, they were the means to national power and wealth.

Liang Qichao, China's foremost modern intellectual, also learned about liberalism and democracy from the leading Meiji interpreters of English liberalism, Fukuzawa Yukichi and Katō Hiroyuki. These Japanese liberals tended to see liberty in terms of its contribution to the Meiji project of *bunmei kaika* (civilisation and enlightenment) rather than in terms of natural, inalienable rights. Advocating a national polity (*kokutai*) centred on the emperor's sovereignty, they emphasised the importance of a strong state in an era of foreign imperialism. Liang followed them in stressing the need to cultivate patriotic citizens who would participate in public life. Individual liberties or natural rights were meaningless in a country that was not independent. The important thing was for the citizens of the new China to be of service to the state, and enable it to withstand the power of Western economic imperialism. In Liang's view, a megalomaniacal businessman like Cecil Rhodes could get away with anything in South Africa because his government backed him. Visiting the US in 1903, Liang feared that American industrial trusts, which he thought more powerful than Alexander the Great and Genghis Khan, would soon cross the Pacific to prey on a weak China. To hold its own, China's agrarian society needed not socialism or free markets but industrial production through capitalist methods, regulated by the state.

Japan, coerced into the international economic order in the middle of the nineteenth century by the arrival of America's 'black ships', had already embarked on an ambitious programme of state-led modernisation, first to resist and then to catch up with the West. Through the policy of *fukoku kyohei* (enrich the country and strengthen the military), it hoped to abandon 'backward' Asia and join 'civilised' Europe. During the civil rights movement of the 1870s, Japan's liberals espoused negative freedom, upholding individual rights against state power, but they also hoped the powerful nation state would advance individual autonomy. Later, in the Taisho period (1912–26), List-reading liberals wanted the state to implement social-welfare policies for the benefit of the working poor: they perceived the inequalities built into modern capitalism, and trusted in the capacity of the state to manage them. They also wanted Japan to enter the international system of competitive imperialism. This drew them into supporting militarism, as the career of the political theorist Yoshino Sakuzō (1878–1933) shows.

In *An Imperial Path to Modernity*, Jung-sun Ni Han describes how Yoshino first developed an idea of the 'organic state' in 1905, at the time of the Russo-Japanese War. Every individual, as he saw it, had to be mobilised for the war effort. He still believed that Japan had to insinuate itself into the Western liberal club. The ideals and institutions of Western Europe had helped facilitate a self-regulating global market with multilateral imperial exchanges. Japan had to fight Russia because it was violating international rules – the Anglo-American framework of open-door imperialism – by trying to create a closed market in Manchuria.

Three years in China and a long stint in Europe brought Yoshino closer to the sources of Western power. Japan, he now saw, lacked the advantages that free-trading Western Europe had accumulated by industrialising and colonising so early: it needed protected markets of its own. China, where all the advanced Western powers already had major stakes, seemed a suitable laboratory for the Japanese experiment in liberal imperialism. Yoshino supported the humiliating Twenty-One

Demands for extraterritorial rights and commercial privileges that Japan presented to China in 1915.

In Japan, Yoshino proposed a political system he called *minpon-shugi*, in which securing the welfare of the people was the purpose of government, and the populace at large participated in the imperial project. As Yoshino saw it, 'it is absolutely necessary to solidify the nation's inner strength through popular awakening.' His scheme, which avoided all notions of popular sovereignty, was directed against oligarchs and bureaucrats indifferent to the population's general welfare. Further rationalisations were marshalled to fortify the liberal project of progress at home and expansion abroad. Yoshino helped popularise the notion that China, which had neither a centralised government nor a developed industrial economy, wasn't yet a proper nation state, and needed to be helped up the evolutionary ladder by Japan. (This was the beginning of the idea of regional 'co-prosperity' later offered to Japan's Asian victims during the Second World War.) Yoshino wasn't advocating a retrograde militarism: he deplored Japanese excesses in China and argued for a more peaceful expansion and consolidation of Japanese interests through local collaboration. He defined Japan's goals in China with reference to liberal philosophies of progress and development.

Such naive loyalty 'to the ideas and social forms of the liberal world order' proved disastrous, first economically then politically, as Mark Metzler recounts in *Lever of Empire: The International Gold Standard and the Crisis of Liberalism in Prewar Japan*. Japan had joined a global financial system run by Britain before the First World War in order to secure Western capital – and diplomatic approval – for its programme of national expansion. But the rules weren't set up for the benefit of 'have-not' powers. 'The hegemony of orthodox Anglo-American ideas of economics', Metzler writes, 'helped to keep Japan in chronic recession in the 1920s.' Japan liberated itself from the system only when it went off the gold standard in

1931 and embraced economic nationalism, reinstating a fully managed currency and comprehensive state controls over trade and industry. 'Other results of this new course', Metzler says, 'were alienation from the West, withdrawal from the League of Nations and, finally, war with the United States and Britain.'

Laments for a never-found 'authentic' liberalism merely point to its contingent nature – in the West as well as the East – and the impossibility of replicating it in adverse socio-economic conditions. The peculiar varieties of liberal thought in Asia reveal the constraints on the political choices open to most of the world's population. They also show that the old normative explanations of the rise of liberal capitalist modernity tend to suppress one of its major enabling factors: imperial domination. Contrary to the claims of its post-war American overlords, Japan's liberal project was shaped rather than doomed by its acquisition of an empire and its absorption of the transnational norms of imperialism along with the rhetoric of progress and development. Its intellectual and political leaders echoed the nineteenth-century European rhetoric of liberalism according to which civilised Europeans brought progress to uncivilised societies, using violence and coercion whenever necessary. Yoshino merely provided a Japanese variation on this 'progressivism' when he justified the abrogation of Chinese sovereignty. His real counterpart, however, is not Mill, who was, after all, the theoriser of a rich, established empire, but Tocqueville, for whom Britain was both rival and model – a country that had raced ahead of its peers in the quest for virtue and glory.

Tocqueville developed his enthusiasm for the colonisation of North Africa after arriving at similar conclusions to Yoshino's: that the growth of a stable and liberal democracy at home might require the exploitation of societies abroad, and that principles of equality and self-determination for conquered peoples would have to be suspended. Unlike English liberals, who sustained a self-serving myth of benevolent empire, Tocqueville allowed himself no illusions about the need for violence:

I have often heard men in France whom I respect, but with whom I do not agree, find it wrong that we burn harvests, that we empty silos, and finally that we seize unarmed men, women and children. These, in my view, are unfortunate necessities, but ones to which any people who want to wage war on the Arabs are obliged to submit.

Japanese liberals as well as militarists felt 'obliged to submit' to such necessities during Japan's savage assault on China in the 1930s. Unfortunately for them, the global race for surplus value and resources, which had underpinned liberalism at home in the West, had already produced its ultimate winners. Liberalism failed in Japan because the country did not already have the power and wealth of the imperial nation state working in its favour, and it was always extremely fragile because, as Raymond Aron put it in *The Opium of the Intellectuals*, nowhere in the West, 'during the long years when industrial populations were growing rapidly, factory chimneys looming up over the suburbs and railways and bridges being constructed, were personal liberties, universal suffrage and the parliamentary system combined'. The modern state in the West was constructed during the decades when 'there were autocratic regimes in which universal suffrage was combined with the absolute power of a single man; there were parliamentary regimes in which the suffrage was restricted and the assembly aristocratic; or there were constitutional monarchies.'

Post-war Asians seemed to have learned these secrets of Western power better than pre-war Japanese liberals. Individualism, laissez-faire economics and a fundamental distrust of state power were discarded everywhere else in Asia in the rush to build and consolidate a strong national buffer against the liberal empires of the West. Confronted with the imperatives of modernisation, most Asian nation states chose protectionist economies and political institutions that put national unity and order before individual rights. Successful economic modernisers, such as Singapore's Lee Kuan Yew and Malaysia's Mahathir Mohamad, claimed in the 1990s that 'Asian values' of social cohesion, thrift and foresight had achieved prosperity more speedily and safely than had liberal individualism.

Even in India, the Asian country most receptive to British political nostrums, liberalism 'did not lead on directly' to democratic government, as Bayly put it: 'until very late, Indian liberals worried about the rapid extension of the franchise.' The left-leaning leaders of the Congress party had begun to recognise by the 1930s that it needed a programme of economic development to attract the peasantry and urban working classes. Nehru institutionalised state initiatives in many areas of public life after assuming power in 1947. The state still has prescriptive powers in the running of the economy, despite two decades of liberalisation. India's impeccably liberal constitution has not produced a liberal political culture. On the contrary, a mass politics based on caste and religious solidarities, in which particular groups rather than individuals are the bearers of rights, undermined the liberal vision of secular, self-interested and rational citizens. The electoral triumph of Narendra Modi, and the collapse of the Gandhi–Nehru dynasty, has infused fresh life into the old Hindu nationalist project of fabricating a modern subject that is assertively Indian in its religious–cultural practices and moral values.

Japan became an American protectorate after the war, with a parliamentary system, and was enlisted in a liberal capitalist order centred on the United States. But its turn to economic nationalism in the early 1930s was never reversed. Japan receives less foreign direct investment as a proportion of its GDP than North Korea, and its economic system today is more closed and centrally organised than it was in the 1910s and 1920s.

But it is China that poses the biggest challenge to Anglo-Americans still hoping to shape the conversation of mankind. Chinese communists systematically overhauled the body politic in order to command loyalty from the people, crushing all individual challenges to the often arbitrary power of the centralised state. Mao's heirs, who allowed China's citizens more room for economic initiative, did not break with the imperatives Liang Qichao had identified: to mobilise China's resources to make it truly autonomous and secure, and to postpone the expansion of individual freedoms. Today, despite extensive marketisation, the state perches on the commanding heights of the globalised economy, encouraging state-owned enterprises and maintaining control of strategic industries.

'Development is the only hard truth,' Deng said. 'If we do not develop, then we will be bullied.' Speaking of the 'China Dream', Xi Jinping asserts the same imperatives of national unity, strength and pride against the need for broad democratic reform. The many micro-freedoms – to consume and travel – increasingly made available to the middle classes help stave off challenges to the authority of the state. Beijing's rhetoric of social welfare still has many more takers than the free-market prescriptions of the country's besieged liberals. Invoking Mao one moment and Confucius the next, for the sake of ideological legitimacy, China's rulers seem no less self-serving than anyone else. But they are not wholly unpersuasive when they present liberalism as an unaffordable plaything of rich Westerners: the elevation into universal values of codes that long favoured a tiny minority and are unlikely to survive the rise of everyone else.

2015

7

The Age of the Crisis of Man

An American Malady

Mark Greif's book is a bracingly ambitious attempt at a 'philosophical history' of the American mid-century, a chronological account of writers and their ideas. It begins in 1933 with an apparently widely perceived 'crisis of man' in American intellectual culture and is cut off, equally surgically, in 1973, with academic theory's announcement of the 'death of man'. Greif, a founding editor of *n+1*, one of the consistently excellent periodicals of the last decade, was drawn to his subject after noticing the number of mid-century American book titles that refer to 'man in crisis': a genre of literature that filled the basement shelves of his childhood, 'the worthy and earnest paperbacks that my parents' generation inherited to educate themselves for the responsibilities of their era'.

A lot of books were indeed published in the United States with the word 'man' in their title (though a taxonomy of crisis literature would also show much anxiety about 'civilisation' and the 'West'). Revealingly, most of these were written by European exiles and expatriates in the US (Fromm, Cassirer, Marcuse, Arendt, Voegelin): their formative intellectual experience was of the economic and political crisis of Europe, and of middle-class attachment to right-wing or downright fascist palliatives. In the US, they observed the domestication of European technologies of control and organisation, and the rapidly changing relationship between machines and men, politics and economics. Greif shows that the crisis-of-man discourse resonated in America in such diverse forms as the post-war cults of Kafka, existentialism and human rights, and in the writings of Dwight Macdonald and Susan Sontag. Thomist theologians were as much a part of it as New York's Jewish intellectuals. 'Man', Greif writes, 'became at mid-century the figure everyone insisted must be addressed, recognised, helped, rescued, made the centre, the measure, the "root".'

Some American writers responded to anxieties about the enfeebling of European liberal humanism with cultural tonics of their own. Lionel Trilling declared after the war that 'the great work of our time is the restoration and reconstitution of . . . the great former will of humanism.' Greif writes insightfully about the canonisation of Hemingway and Faulkner, and the careful packaging of US soft power: the 'nation's individualism, its energy, its religious darkness, its democracy, its philosophical depth to rival Europe, and its fecundity'. He examines *The Adventures of Augie March*, *The Crying of Lot 49* and *Wise Blood*, books 'in which the new authority of unmarked, universal man could be borrowed and spread, and yet where its contradictions and gaps would come into relief'. His analysis of *Invisible Man* is particularly original. And ending his philosophical history in 1973 makes sense, even though the American idea of man as *homo economicus* has accumulated more ideological power in the four decades since. In the 1960s European structuralists and deconstructionists were already expressing doubts about a 'tyrannical universal', doubts which were then amplified on Ivy League campuses and in some American literary fiction. In the broader countercultural revolt, women and members of racial, ethnic and sexual minorities denounced the premises behind universal manhood – progress, sovereignty, free will, moral truth, reason – as exclusivist and self-serving creations of white, heterosexual bourgeois males. In the regime of deindustrialisation and globalised financial capitalism that followed the oil crisis of 1973, man would be increasingly deprived of his work ethic (and self-worth) and burdened by unprecedented professional risk and existential uncertainty, to the point, now reached, where only Davos Man – the hyper-connected embodiment of capitalism – appears to possess a special being and authority.

Greif moves nimbly from *Being and Nothingness* to Edward Steichen's Family of Man exhibition at MoMA and the Universal Declaration of Human Rights. Yet his way of weaving a network of resemblances and discontinuities together, along with his evident gift for paraphrase and summary, might lead the reader to expect something less dispassionate and more focused: a controlling argument rather than a series of episodes and vignettes. *The Age of the Crisis of Man* seems at first to be a rich genealogy, like Samuel Moyn's *The Last Utopia*, which describes the way the concept of 'human rights', beginning in the 1940s, eclipsed social and economic rights before becoming part of the rhetorical arsenal of freedom promoters and humanitarian interventionists. Or like Udi Greenberg's recent book, *The Weimar Century: German Emigrés and the Ideological Foundations of the Cold War*, which blends intellectual with political history in its account of the making of the government–academic nexus in mid-century America. But Greif turns out to be an inquisitive and nostalgic curator of his family's bookshelves and graduate seminar texts, and a stimulating literary critic, rather than a social historian or intellectual archaeologist. He refuses to judge whether the discourse of the crisis of man was 'wise, or either good or bad', and says he is more interested in 'the proliferation of answers, not their conclusion'. But only a reader attuned to the parochial assumptions of American exceptionalism will find anything remarkable in the fact that so many mid-century Europeans or Euro-Americans were obsessed with the crisis of man.

Crisis in general defined the decades from the First World War to the Holocaust – closing time for many in the gardens of the West. Intellectual and artistic modernism emerged in

Europe out of an attempt to describe, diagnose and often celebrate the breakdown of the nineteenth century's verities about post-Enlightenment man. By the early twentieth century the aggressive bourgeois ego which George Santayana saw emerge in the industrialising US – the go-getting American with no higher aim than diligent imitation of the rich – was already under siege in Europe by oversized and complex political and economic systems. Sociologists had identified fresh threats to human autonomy in capitalist rationalisation and bureaucratisation. 'Each man', Weber warned, 'becomes a little cog in the machine', pathetically obsessed with becoming 'a bigger cog'. Karel Čapek invented the word 'robot', deriving it from the Czech word for forced labour, to evoke the growing superfluity of man in the regime of technology. The slaughter of the First World War seemed to confirm that, as Franz Rosenzweig put it, 'reason' had 'devoured' man. An artilleryman in the war, he had seen 'man creep like a worm into the folds of the naked earth': 'His *I* would be but an *It* if he died.' Embracing the 'god of destruction', Count Psanek in D. H. Lawrence's post-war story *The Ladybird* expresses the nihilistic rage that overcame many superfluous men then and since. 'God has put the hammer in my breast,' Psanek announces, sounding like one of Islamic State's flashy executioners and vandals. 'It hits on the world of man. It hits, it hits! And it hears the thin sound of cracking.'

This sound, echoing among disaffected masses in Europe and Asia throughout the twentieth century, didn't reach the US until early in the twenty-first century. What fatefully isolates the American experience, and much American reflection on it, is that the US enjoyed an extraordinary growth in military and economic power during the two world wars that levelled much of Europe and Asia. This national expansion at a time of worldwide trauma and mayhem is what makes the US truly exceptional (and explains, among other things, the striking absence of a sense of tragedy and limit in its geopolitical schemes, and the invincible can-doism of its politicians and publicists). In Europe, the nineteenth century's certainties – primary among them Western universalism, the old Jewish–Christian claim to be able to create a life of universal validity now transposed into secular millenarianism – had been undermined by historical calamities and blistering critiques from across the ideological spectrum. Lévi-Strauss and Sartre both concluded that Enlightenment universalism had turned into a form of racism, 'an attempt to wipe out the diversity of cultures while pretending to accord it full recognition'. Carl Schmitt claimed that whoever invokes humanity, 'an especially useful ideological instrument of imperialist expansion', 'wants to cheat'. Yet the post-war years in the US witnessed the ideological redefinition of such abstract concepts as 'freedom', 'democracy', 'human rights' and indeed 'man'; the restored will of liberal humanism, boosted by American capitalism, tried to rescue Europe's universalist philosophies of history and progress from discredit.

Modernisation along American lines now became the creed that glorified the sovereign liberty of the autonomous rights-bearing man and hailed his rational choice-making capacity as freedom. A century and a half after Stendhal denounced the materialism of the French bourgeoisie, economic growth in general was posited as the end-all of political life and the chief marker of progress worldwide. Unlike in the 1820s, those who claimed that a culture of money-making advanced the freedom of man could now depend on a useful enemy. Communism was totalitarian. Ergo its ideological opponent, American liberalism, represented freedom. This evangelical Americanism was assisted not only by the 'militant Christian' belief, as Norman Mailer described it, that America is 'the only force for good that can rectify the bad'. America's presumed leadership of the free world also bred an atmosphere of solemn conformity among many of its expensively educated middle-class and secular-minded beneficiaries. In no other country did a generation voluntarily read worthy and earnest books to learn about its responsibilities to man.

Many writers after 1945 reflected searchingly on the murky ambiguities of unprecedented national and individual success. Greif engagingly discusses some of these (Niebuhr, Baldwin, Chomsky) while puzzlingly omitting, among others, Christopher Lasch, who offered sustained critiques of the peculiarly American reconfigurations of the idea of universal man. Those capable of really examining the power elites and the culture of narcissism – and the oracles warning against the fire next time – were always going to be marginal in a society designed to maximise productivity and profit. The truly influential texts about human possibility in this period weren't Dwight Macdonald's *The Root Is Man* or even the widely read *The Organisation Man* by William Whyte, but Walt Rostow's *The Stages of Economic Growth: A Non-communist Manifesto* and Daniel Boorstin's *The Genius of American Politics*. What happened in such journals of modest circulation as *Politics* and *Partisan Review* was politically negligible compared to the efforts of the *New Republic*, whose eloquent mea culpa in January about its dishonourable treatment of racial inequity doesn't quite obscure the fact that generations of boosters of American exceptionalism flourished in its pages, in convenient proximity to the Pentagon. 'The American discourse of the crisis of man in general was surprisingly oblivious to colonial thinking,' Greif writes, and to the futures after the Second World War of the 'colonial, soon-to-be postcolonial, peoples'. The word 'surprisingly' is superfluous here. The crisis of man in post-war America was almost exclusively a white man's discourse, an affirmation of his privilege to define the ends and means of life without being bothered by women and non-whites; the rare outsider they listened to, such as Ralph Ellison, concluded, as Greif points out, that universal humanity in a universal history 'makes ruined buildings, and dead men'.

Greif knows that the American interrogation of the crisis of man was programmed to receive 'a single inductive or deductive answer'. But his aims are both too ambitious and too modest. Based on a limited selection of mid-century figures and texts, his history neither traces the crisis of man to its roots in Europe nor broadens out to show how a fundamentally derivative discourse was diffused, translated and consumed in another socio-economic and geopolitical context – that of an imperial power making the world safe for consumer capitalism. 'What the mid-century intellectuals really tried to launch', he writes, 'was an autochthonous humanism – human respect giving its grounds entirely to itself, without God, natural law, positive fiat, or even anything identifiable about the human person like "rationality".' Thus also spoke Zarathustra in 1882. However, the *Übermensch* in post-war America was too prone to simulating an autochthonous humanism in patriotic mode, and too keen to press it on other countries. Or – the alternative – to retreat, in the neo-liberal age, into the care of the self through yoga, meditation and diet programmes. Edward Mendelson, a practitioner of the nearly lost art of biographical criticism, has shrewd things to say in *Moral Agents* about white male writers struggling with the inflated sense of national and individual capacity in the land of the free. American intellectuals, Van Wyck Brooks claimed in *America's Coming of Age*, are a 'race of Hamlets', 'acutely conscious of their spiritual unemployment and impoverished in will and impulse'. Many artists and intellectuals who came of age in a wealthy and powerful country after the Second World War found themselves released from spiritual unemployment; they suddenly had an unprecedented freedom to realise personal ambitions, forge identities and control their destinies.

But such beneficiaries of America's post-war plentitude were also condemned to the psychic strain of managing public personas, assessing self-images and calibrating their place in a society ceaselessly on the make. Saul Bellow's fiction repeatedly bemoans the haplessness of eggheads in the garish drama of American-style freedom and democracy. Mendelson shows how some prominent writers actually enacted, as well as writing about, the crisis of man in America. The most surprising victim in *Moral Agents* is Lionel Trilling, the putative rebuilder of American humanism, whose 'amoral, nihilistic inner self kept resolving to repudiate his outer self's "character of public virtue".' Mendelson, who has read Trilling's unpublished journals, hints that his reservations about a complacent liberal imagination may have emerged from painful self-awareness – even self-disgust. The thought that he had 'one of the great reputations in the academic world' made him 'retch'. Envious of Hemingway, and harried by his wife, Diana, Trilling confessed periodically to 'the panic and emptiness which make their onset when the will is tired from its own excess'.

With delicate precision, Mendelson traces similar private confusion and anxiety in Trilling's coevals. Alfred Kazin marvelled in his journals at his own social and intellectual eminence – its high-water mark a lunch invitation to the White House – and sexual success. Unlike Trilling, he sublimates self-contempt into scorn for the neocons dying to break bread with the president. Numerous prizes, marriages and affairs didn't prevent Bellow from being driven, according to Mendelson, 'throughout his life by his search for some ultimate and invisible spiritual reality'. Augie March, commonly assumed to be a self-made American hero, appears in Bellow's own conception as a classic authoritarian personality, eager to serve external authority and discipline: 'To me,' Bellow wrote in one of his letters, 'Augie is the embodiment of willingness to serve, who says "For God's sake, make use of me, only do not use me to no purpose." . . . Surely the greatest human desire . . . is to be used.' In his own quasi-masochistic reverence for the anthroposophy of Rudolf Steiner, Bellow achieved a startling resemblance to Allen Ginsberg prostrate before Tibetan lamas.

Indeed, the most intriguing revelation in Mendelson's book is how often his 'moral agents' turned from secular temptations of wealth, fame and sex to religious consolations and interpretations. Auden's Christianity was 'a product of his deracinated life in America, at first deeply interior and intellectualised'. As for Mailer, the 'mystical prophet thundering against technology', human beings always appeared to him as embodiments of 'quasi-divine forces', rather than as agents of rational self-interest. He saw 'authority and nihilism stalking one another in the orgiastic hollow of this century', and predictably took a theological view of 9/11: 'Gods and demons were invading the US, coming right in off the TV screen . . . It was as if untold divine forces were erupting in fury.' But what – apart from the debasing inescapability of money and the temptation of power – explains the fact, revealed in his recently published journals, that Kazin was engrossed 'from adolescence' in 'a spiritual and sometimes mystical inner life'? Marcuse had argued in the 1960s that alternative values to triumphant capitalism, which had eliminated the possibility of revolution, could only emerge from desires – for inner peace, for instance – that were manifestly frustrated by capitalist rationality. It seems that spirituality became, in late capitalist Manhattan as much as in the shah's Iran, the heart of a heartless world – the opium of an intellectual elite as well as of the people.

Cloistered piety was definitely a better option, in America at least, than the intoxicant of power: the 'allure of joining the powerful', which, Greif observes, can feel 'superior to the satisfactions of being undeceived and critical (and struggling always from the margins)'. During the Cold War, many intellectuals, on the left as well as the right, chose to become members of a privileged class, even eager dispensers of technocratic wisdom to financial and political power, and rationalisers of imperial warmaking. The most egregious examples of the Beltway sage today seem to be the neoconservative exponents of deregulation at home and freedom in the Middle East: 'arrivistes', in Mendelson's judgement, who 'identified their own success' in post-war America with 'eternal moral truths'. The trend actually dates back to the mid-century high point of American liberalism. Kazin was already worried during the Vietnam War about 'the stake that so many intellectuals now have in the inequalities of our society', and 'the extent to which we are implicated in our wars as in our prosperity'.

Though doused in Saigon in 1975, a retro nineteenth-century craving for universal mastery and control was rekindled in 1989 among many members of what Tony Judt called the 'crappy generation' – the one that 'grew up in the 1960s in Western Europe or in America, in a world of no hard choices, neither economic nor political'. Judt's indictment extended beyond Bush, the Clintons, Blair and neocon publicists to intellectuals at the 'traditional liberal centre' – the *New Yorker*, the *New Republic*, the *Washington Post* and the *New York Times* – who, he wrote, had turned into a 'service class'. Researching his book in 2003, Greif seems to have been troubled by this spectacle. Liberal intellectuals who might have been interested in his book about the crisis of man were, he writes, 'busy preparing the justification of the US invasion of Iraq . . . on the basis of a renewed anthropological vision of "who we are" (in the West) against a new "they" figured as totalitarian'. Greif, who spent his intellectually formative years watching liberals applaud Clinton's triangulations and Bush's crusades, knows that the crappy generation's grand self-images can no longer be sustained. Over the last decade, military setbacks, political turpitude and economic disasters have inadvertently completed the provincialisation of universal man undertaken by post-humanist theory. The old fantasies about man as the maker of history and the master of nature now return as parody among the gaudily virile American centurions and climate-change deniers of Republican presidential primaries. And so Greif cautions gently on the last page, 'Anytime your inquiries lead you to say, "At this moment we must ask and decide *who we fundamentally are* . . ." just stop.'

But Greif has not built a solid case in the preceding, politically neutral, pages; many of his would-be interlocutors are likely to misidentify him as a reluctant liberal. Praising *The Age of the Crisis of Man* in the *New York Times*, Leon Wieseltier, the former literary editor of the *New Republic*, came out for old-style liberal universalism: 'Don't just stop,' he exhorted. 'Think harder. Get it right. (Why are liberals so afraid of their own philosophy?)' Michael Walzer, co-editor of *Dissent*, recently issued a call to arms against radical Islam even though the US has already helped ignite wars in several Muslim countries: 'So here I am, a writer, not a fighter,' he urged, 'and the most helpful thing I can do is to join the ideological wars.'

Greif is wary of precisely this kind of 'sermonising about responsibility, urgency and hapless prescription' that has long made liberal universalists indistinguishable from neocon arrivistes. Nevertheless, intellectuals who portentously embraced their responsibilities to man during the Cold War can't but depend even more on negative definitions – of Islam now – as Iraq and its environs descend deeper into havoc, and as aspects of the twentieth century's much-despised communist states resurface in the free world: inefficient and uncontrolled economies, expensive and failing welfare systems, vast surveillance mechanisms, and a state that has subordinated civil liberties to perpetual warfare against real and imagined enemies. The legal limbo of Guantánamo and extra-judicial murder by drone has realised the most vivid nightmares dreamed during the mid-century American cult of Kafka. The fact of deepening and irreversible inequality is aggravated by the awareness that there is nothing on offer to replace an ideology that promises freedom and progress through endless economic expansion and technological innovation. American pathologies – extreme concentrations of wealth, criminalisation of the poor, rogue security establishments, corrupted and dysfunctional politics and a compliant media – have been universalised, much more successfully than democracy and human rights.

Homo economicus, who seeks to replace all other human values and interests with cost–benefit calculations, rampages across the globe: in personal relations as well as the workplace, higher education and political institutions. Pulverising the welfarist state, and even a sense of community, and contemptuous of history and tradition, he sentences hundreds of millions to economic and psychological insecurity and isolation in an opaque and hostile world. This scorched-earth universalism incites, as Santayana warned, 'a lava-wave of primitive blindness and violence'. Many putative Augie Marches, whether in India, Russia, Japan or Israel, seem keen to surrender their onerous individuality to demagogues and to be used by them. Elsewhere, those excluded from a degraded world of man, or condemned to join its burgeoning precariat, are prone to embrace the god of destruction rather than of inner peace. The thin sound of cracking is heard from many more parts of the world as exhausted authority surrenders to nihilism.

2015

8

Free Markets and Social Darwinism in Mumbai

On Katharine Boo

In *The Drowned and the Saved*, Primo Levi describes an experience that fatally undermined many of his fellow condemned at Auschwitz. Entering the death camp, he had hoped, he wrote, 'at least for the solidarity of one's companions in misfortune'. Instead, there were 'a thousand sealed-off monads, and between them a desperate covert and continuous struggle'. This was what Levi called the 'Gray Zone', where the 'network of human relationships' 'could not be reduced to the two blocs of victims and persecutors', and where 'the enemy was all around but also inside'.

It may seem grotesquely inappropriate to recall Levi's struggles for survival in a Nazi camp while thinking of the apparently self-reliant individualists of a slum called Annawadi near Mumbai's airport – the setting of Katherine Boo's extraordinary first book, which describes a few months in the life of a young garbage trader, Abdul, and his friends and family. After all, these plucky 'slumdogs' may be – in at least one recent fantasy – India's next millionaires, part of the lucky 1 per cent able to savour the five-star hotels that loom over Annawadi. As noted by Boo – a staff writer at the *New Yorker* who was awarded the Pulitzer Prize for public service in 2000, when she was a journalist at the *Washington Post* – they are not considered poor by 'official' Indian benchmarks; they are 'among roughly

100 million Indians freed from poverty since 1991', when the central government 'embraced economic liberalization', 'part of one of the most stirring success narratives in the modern history of global market capitalism', in which a self-propelling economic system is geared to reward motivated and resourceful individuals with personal wealth.

Indeed, hope is a more common intoxicant in Annawadi than the discarded bottles of Eraz-ex (the Indian equivalent of Wite-Out) inhaled by Abdul's scavenger friends. The slum dwellers speak 'of better lives casually, as if fortune were a cousin arriving on Sunday, as if the future would look nothing like the past'. Yet, as Boo details, 'for every two people in Annawadi inching up, there was one in a catastrophic plunge'.

Many of the slum dwellers, including Abdul, gain their sense of upward mobility by contrasting their lot with that of their less fortunate neighbours, 'miserable souls' who 'trapped rats and frogs and fried them for dinner' or 'ate the scrub grass at the sewage lake's edge'. Migrants fleeing a crisis-ridden agricultural sector cause an oversupply of cheap labour in Mumbai, so the boy whose hand is sliced off by a shredding machine turns, 'with his blood-spurting stump', to assure his boss that he won't report the accident.

A two-year-old girl drowns suspiciously in a pail, and a father empties a pot of boiling lentils over his sick baby. As Boo explains, 'sickly children of both sexes were sometimes done away with, because of the ruinous cost of their care'. 'Young girls in the slums', she adds, 'died all the time under dubious circumstances, since most slum families couldn't afford the sonograms that allowed wealthier families to dispose of their female liabilities before birth.'

Adults, too, drop like flies. One of Abdul's friends ends up as a corpse with his eyes gouged out. Injured men bleed to death, unattended, by the road to the airport. Maggots breed in the infected sores of the scavengers Boo hangs out with. 'Gangrene inched up fingers, calves swelled into tree trunks, and Abdul and his younger brothers kept a running wager about which of the scavengers would be the next to die.'

These continual human losses are taken mostly in a matter-of-fact way in Annawadi. For Abdul and his friends have 'accepted the basic truths: that in a modernizing, increasingly prosperous city, their lives were embarrassments best confined to small spaces, and their deaths would matter not at all'.

Those deaths might even get the survivors into trouble. So when the one-legged Fatima, Abdul's querulous neighbour, sets herself on fire, a small crowd gathers but does nothing: 'The adults drifted back to their dinners, while a few boys waited to see if Fatima's face would come off.' Trying to take Fatima to the hospital, her husband finds himself shunned by autorickshaw drivers, who are worried about 'the potential damage to seat covers'.

As for the nearby policemen, they embody pure terror in the eyes of Annawadians. They won't balk at raping a homeless girl, and would 'gladly blow their noses in your last piece of bread'. The police actually encourage Fatima to blame Abdul's family so that officers can extort money from them. A government officer threatens to collect false witness statements unless she is paid off.

Neither India's hollowed-out democracy nor its mean-minded new capitalism, which cannot do without a helot class, seems able to relieve this social-Darwinist brutishness. Far from being a testimony to the audacity of hope, the dauntless human spirit and that kind of thing, Annawadi turns out to be a grey zone whose atomised residents want nothing more than, in Primo Levi's words, 'to preserve and consolidate' their 'established privilege vis-à-vis those without privilege'. Even those who are relatively fortunate, Boo writes, 'improved their lots by beggaring the life chances of other poor people'.

Describing this undercity blood sport, *Behind the Beautiful Forevers* (the ironic title is taken from the 'Beautiful Forever' advertisements for Italianate floor tiles that hide Annawadi from view) does not descend into a catalogue of atrocity – one that a defensive Indian nationalist might dismiss as a drain inspector's report. The product of prolonged and risky self-exposure to Annawadi, the book's narrative stitches, with much skilfully unspoken analysis, some carefully researched individual lives. Its considerable literary power is also derived from Boo's soberly elegant prose, which only occasionally reaches for exuberant neologism ('Glimmerglass Hyatt') and bright metaphor ('Each evening, they returned down the slum road with gunny sacks of garbage on their backs, like a procession of broken-toothed, profit-minded Santas').

But *Behind the Beautiful Forevers* is, above all, a moral inquiry in the great tradition of Oscar Lewis and Michael Harrington. As Boo explains in an author's note, the spectacle of Mumbai's 'profound and juxtaposed inequality' provoked a line of questioning: 'What is the infrastructure of opportunity in this society? Whose capabilities are given wing by the market and a government's economic and social policy? Whose capabilities are squandered? . . . Why don't more of our unequal societies implode?' Her eye is as shrewdly trained on the essential facts of politics and commerce as on the intimate, the familial and, indeed, the monstrously absurd: the college-going girl who struggles to figure out 'Mrs Dalloway' while her closest friend, about to be forced into an arranged marriage, consumes rat poison, and dies (though not before the doctors attending her extort 5,000 rupees, or $100, from her parents).

You wonder, intermittently, about the book's omniscient narrator. Perhaps wisely, Boo has absented herself from her narrative. The story of how a white American journalist overcame the suspicion of her subjects (and the outright hostility of the police), or dealt with the many ethical conundrums created by close contact between the First and Fourth Worlds, belongs to another book. Instead of the *faux naïf* explainer or the intrepid adventurer in Asian badlands, you get a reflective sensibility, subtly informing every page with previous experiences of deprivation and striving, and a gentle scepticism about ideological claims.

Boo can see how democracy, routinely lauded in the West as India's great advantage over authoritarian China, can be turned into yet another insider network of patronage in which the powerful flourish: how periodic elections can be absorbed into 'a national game of make-believe, in which many of India's old problems – poverty, disease, illiteracy, child labor – were being aggressively addressed', even as 'exploitation of the weak by the less weak continued with minimal interference'.

She can also perceive why many well-off Indians have grown impatient with, even contemptuous of, democracy and, like their counterparts elsewhere, want to eliminate rather than enhance the social-welfarist obligations of government. For these Indians, Boo points out, 'private security was hired, city water was filtered, private school tuitions were paid. Such choices had evolved over the years into a principle: The best government is the one that gets out of the way.'

Boo deftly steers clear of the many banal notions about corruption in India unleashed recently by a quasi-Gandhian protest movement supported by affluent Indians. She shows how corruption, far from being a malignant external growth, is integral to India's political, economic and social system. 'Among powerful Indians,' she writes, 'the distribution of opportunity was typically an insider trade.' And for the 'poor of a country where corruption thieved a great deal of opportunity, corruption was one of the genuine opportunities that remained'.

Fully inhabiting India's troubled present, *Behind the Beautiful Forevers* can only hint at a less oppressive past – a 'peaceful age' that to Abdul sounds like something out of myth, a time when 'poor people had accepted the fates that their respective gods had written on their foreheads, and in turn treated one another more kindly.' This may seem too romantic a picture of oriental fatalism. It is true, nevertheless, that migrants from the rural hinterland, drawn to Mumbai for hundreds of years – as long as the city, as constructed by British free-traders and their native collaborators, has existed – were never as desolate and defenceless as they are now.

So much of the city's most popular exports – cinema and music – originated in the past from the attempt by rural migrants to re-create, in the big alienating city, the traditions of their lost community. But unlike Mumbai's previous generation of migrants, Annawadians cannot have any soothing dreams of a return to village life and its communal solidarities. Boo makes this clear in a brisk digression to a rural region of western India where thousands of farmers, forced out of a subsistence economy into a globalised one, have killed themselves in the previous decade.

Here, many citizens have not only 'stopped believing the government's promises about improving their fortunes'. As Boo explains,

> Deprived of their land and historical livelihoods by large-scale corporate and government modernization projects, they'd helped revive a 40-year-old movement of Maoist revolutionaries. Employing land mines, rocket launchers, nail bombs and guns against capitalism and the Indian state, the guerrillas were now at work in roughly one-third of India's 627 districts.

The Maoists seem a weirdly anachronistic intrusion in the 'great success narrative of capitalism'. But for them, as much as for the corporations and governments dispossessing the Indians in the countryside, life in the contemporary world has turned into a zero-sum game. Not surprisingly, Abdul's mother, too, has 'raised her son for a modern age of ruthless competition. In this age, some people rose and some people fell, and ever since he was little, she'd made him understand that he had to rise'.

As Boo shows in wrenching detail, however, Abdul's training turns out to be incomplete. Falsely accused of murdering his neighbour, and fully exposed to a 'malign' justice system, Abdul learns that 'his mother hadn't prepared him for what it felt like, falling alone.'

The ostensible 'rise' of India has attracted its share of literary and journalistic buccaneers in recent years. Unlike China (unlovably aloof, even menacing), India, with its eager English-speakers and periodic elections, is easier to slot into a Western narrative of progress. Thus most recent books about the country, unselfconsciously suffused with the clichés of the age, speak of how free-market capitalism has ignited a general explosion of opportunity, fostering hope among the most destitute of Indians.

Boo describes what happens when opportunity accrues to the already privileged in the age of globalisation, governments remain dysfunctional and corrupt, and, with most citizens locked into a fantasy of personal wealth and consumption, hope, too, is privatised, sundered from any notions of collective well-being.

In this sense, *Behind the Beautiful Forevers* is not just about India's delusory new culture of aspiration. For as Boo writes, 'what was unfolding in Mumbai was unfolding elsewhere, too' – in Nairobi and Santiago, Washington and New York. 'In the age of global market capitalism, hopes and grievances were narrowly conceived, which blunted a sense of common predicament'.

'The poor', she explains further, 'blame one another for the choices of governments and markets, and we who are not poor are ready to blame the poor just as harshly.' Meanwhile, only 'the faintest ripple' is created 'in the fabric of the society at large', for in places like Mumbai, 'the gates of the rich . . . remained unbreached . . . the poor took down one another, and the world's great, unequal cities soldiered on in relative peace.' In its own quiet way, *Behind the Beautiful Forevers* disturbs this peace more effectively than many works of polemic and theory. Transcending its geographical setting, the book also provides a bracing antidote to the ideological opiates of recent decades – those that made the worldwide proliferation of gray zones appear part of a 'great success narrative'.

2012

9

The Lure of Fascist Mysticism

On Jordan Peterson

'Men have to toughen up,' Jordan Peterson writes in *12 Rules for Life: An Antidote to Chaos*. 'Men demand it, and women want it.' So, the first rule is, 'Stand up straight with your shoulders back' and don't forget to 'clean your room'. By the way, 'consciousness is symbolically masculine and has been since the beginning of time.' Oh, and 'the soul of the individual eternally hungers for the heroism of genuine Being.' Many such pronouncements – didactic as well as metaphysical, ranging from the absurdity of political correctness to the 'burden of Being' – have turned Peterson, a professor of psychology at the University of Toronto, into a YouTube sensation and a bestselling author in several Western countries.

12 Rules for Life is only Peterson's second book in twenty years. Packaged for people brought up on *BuzzFeed* listicles, Peterson's brand of intellectual populism has risen with stunning velocity, and it is boosted, like the political populisms of our time, by predominantly male and frenzied followers, who seem ever-ready to pummel his critics on social media. It is imperative to ask why and how this obscure Canadian academic, who insists that gender and class hierarchies are ordained by nature and validated by science, has suddenly come to be hailed as the West's most influential public intellectual. For his apotheosis speaks of a crisis that is at least as deep as the one signified by Donald Trump's unexpected leadership of the free world.

Peterson diagnoses this crisis as a loss of faith in old verities. 'In the West,' he writes, 'we have been withdrawing from our tradition-, religion- and even nation-centred cultures.' Peterson offers to alleviate the resulting 'desperation of meaninglessness', with a return to 'ancient wisdom'. It is possible to avoid 'nihilism', he asserts, and 'to find sufficient meaning in individual consciousness and experience' with the help of 'the great myths and religious stories of the past'.

Following Carl Jung, Peterson identifies 'archetypes' in myths, dreams and religions, which have apparently defined truths of the human condition since the beginning of time. 'Culture', one of his typical arguments goes, 'is symbolically, archetypally, mythically male' – and this is why resistance to male dominance is unnatural. Men represent order, and 'Chaos – the unknown – is symbolically associated with the feminine'. In other words, men resisting the perennially fixed archetypes of male and female, and failing to toughen up, are pathetic losers.

Such evidently eternal truths are not on offer any more at a modern university; Jung's speculations have been largely discredited. But Peterson, armed with his 'maps of meaning' (the title of his previous book), has only contempt for his fellow academics who tend to emphasise the socially constructed and provisional nature of our perceptions. As with Jung, he presents some idiosyncratic quasi-religious opinions as empirical science, frequently appealing to evolutionary psychology to support his ancient wisdom.

Closer examination, however, reveals Peterson's ageless insights as a typical, if not archetypal, product of our own times: right-wing pieties seductively mythologised for our current lost generations.

Peterson himself credits his intellectual awakening to the Cold War, when he began to ponder deeply such 'evils associated with belief' as Hitler, Stalin and Mao, and became a close reader of Solzhenitsyn's *The Gulag Archipelago*. This is a common intellectual trajectory among Western right-wingers who swear by

Solzhenitsyn and tend to imply that belief in egalitarianism leads straight to the guillotine or the Gulag. A recent example is the English polemicist Douglas Murray, who deplores the attraction of the young to Bernie Sanders and Elizabeth Warren and wishes that the idea of equality was 'tainted by an ideological ordure equivalent to that heaped on the concept of borders'. Peterson confirms his membership of this far-right sect by never identifying the evils caused by belief in profit, or Mammon: slavery, genocide and imperialism.

Reactionary white men will surely be thrilled by Peterson's loathing for 'social justice warriors' and his claim that divorce laws should not have been liberalised in the 1960s. Those embattled against political correctness on university campuses will heartily endorse Peterson's claim that 'there are whole disciplines in universities forthrightly hostile towards men'. Islamophobes will take heart from his speculation that 'feminists avoid criticizing Islam because they unconsciously long for masculine dominance'. Libertarians will cheer Peterson's glorification of the individual striver and his stern message to the left-behinds – 'Maybe it's not the world that's at fault. Maybe it's you. You've failed to make the mark.' The demagogues of our age don't read much; but, as they ruthlessly crack down on refugees and immigrants, they can derive much philosophical backup from Peterson's sub-chapter headings: 'Compassion as a vice' and 'Toughen up, you weasel'.

In all respects, Peterson's ancient wisdom is unmistakably modern. The 'tradition' he promotes stretches no further back than the late nineteenth century, when there first emerged a sinister correlation between intellectual exhortations to toughen up and strongmen politics. This was a period during which intellectual quacks flourished by hawking creeds of redemption and purification while political and economic crises deepened and faith in democracy and capitalism faltered. Many artists and thinkers – ranging from the German philosopher Ludwig Klages, member of the hugely influential Munich Cosmic Circle, to the Russian painter Nicholas Roerich and Indian activist Aurobindo Ghosh – assembled Peterson-style collages of part-occultist, part-psychological and part-biological notions. These neo-Romantics were responding, in the same way as Peterson, to an urgent need, springing from a traumatic experience of social and economic modernity, to believe – in whatever reassures and comforts.

This new object of belief tended to be exotically and esoterically premodern. The East, and India in particular, turned into a screen on which needy Westerners projected their fantasies; Jung, among many others, went on tediously about the Indian's timeless – and feminine – self. In 1910, Romain Rolland summed up the widespread mood in which progress under liberal auspices appeared a sham, and many people appeared eager to replace the Enlightenment ideal of individual reason by such transcendental coordinates as 'archetypes'. 'The gate of dreams had reopened,' Rolland wrote, and 'in the train of religion came little puffs of theosophy, mysticism, esoteric faith, occultism to visit the chambers of the Western mind'.

A range of intellectual entrepreneurs, from Theosophists and vendors of Asian spirituality like Vivekananda and D. T. Suzuki to scholars of Asia like Arthur Waley and fascist ideologues like Julius Evola (Steve Bannon's guru), set up stalls in the new marketplace of ideas. W. B. Yeats, adjusting Indian philosophy to the needs of the Celtic Revival, pontificated on the 'Ancient Self'; Jung spun his own variations on this evidently ancestral unconscious. Such conceptually foggy categories as 'spirit' and 'intuition' acquired broad currency; Peterson's favorite words, 'being' and 'chaos', started to appear in capital letters. Peterson's own lineage among these healers of modern man's soul can be traced through his repeatedly invoked influences: not only Carl Jung, but also Mircea Eliade, the Romanian scholar of religion, and Joseph Campbell, a professor at Sarah Lawrence College, who, like Peterson, combined a conventional academic career with mass-market musings on heroic individuals.

The 'desperation of meaninglessness' widely felt in the late nineteenth century seemed especially desperate in the years following two world wars and the Holocaust. Jung, Eliade and Campbell, all credentialled by university education, met a general bewilderment by suggesting the existence of a secret, almost gnostic, knowledge of the world. Claiming to throw light into recessed places in the human unconscious, they acquired immense and fanatically loyal fan clubs. Campbell's 1988 television interviews with Bill Moyers provoked a particularly extraordinary response. As with Peterson, this populariser of archaic myths, who believed that 'Marxist philosophy had overtaken the university in America', was remarkably in tune with contemporary prejudices. 'Follow your own bliss,' he urged an audience that, during an era of neoconservative upsurge, was ready to be reassured that some profound ancient wisdom lay behind Ayn Rand's paeans to unfettered individualism.

Peterson, however, seems to have modelled his public persona on Jung rather than Campbell. The Swiss sage sported a ring ornamented with the effigy of a snake – the symbol of light in a pre-Christian Gnostic cult. Peterson claims that he has been inducted into 'the coastal Pacific Kwakwaka'wakw tribe'; he is clearly proud of the Native American longhouse he has built in his Toronto home.

Peterson may seem the latest in a long line of eggheads pretentiously but harmlessly romancing the noble savage. But it is worth remembering that Jung recklessly generalised about the superior 'Aryan soul' and the inferior 'Jewish psyche' and was initially sympathetic to the Nazis. Mircea Eliade was a devotee of Romania's fascistic Iron Guard. Campbell's loathing of 'Marxist' academics at his college concealed a virulent loathing of Jews and blacks. Solzhenitsyn, Peterson's revered mentor, was a zealous Russian expansionist, who denounced Ukraine's independence and hailed Vladimir Putin as the right man to lead Russia's overdue regeneration.

Nowhere in his published writings does Peterson reckon with the moral fiascos of his gurus and their political ramifications; he seems unbothered by the fact that thinking of human relations in such terms as dominance and hierarchy connects too easily with such nascent viciousness such as misogyny, anti-Semitism and Islamophobia. He might argue that his maps of meaning aim at helping lost individuals rather than racists, ultra-nationalists or imperialists. But he can't plausibly claim, given his oft-expressed hostility to the 'murderous equity doctrine' of feminists, and other progressive ideas, that he is above the fray of our ideological and culture wars.

Indeed, the modern fascination with myth has never been free from an illiberal and anti-democratic agenda. Richard Wagner, along with many German nationalists, became notorious for using myth to regenerate the *Volk* and stoke hatred of the aliens – largely Jews – whom he thought polluted the pure community rooted in blood and soil. By the early twentieth century, ethnic–racial chauvinists everywhere – Hindu supremacists in India as well as Catholic ultra-nationalists in France – were offering visions to uprooted peoples of a rooted organic society in which hierarchies and values had been stable. As Karla Poewe points out in *New Religions and the Nazis*, political cultists would typically mix 'pieces of Yogic and Abrahamic traditions' with 'popular notions of science – or rather pseudo-science – such as concepts of "race," "eugenics," or "evolution."' It was this opportunistic amalgam of ideas that helped nourish 'new mythologies of would-be totalitarian regimes'.

Peterson rails today against 'softness', arguing that men have been 'pushed too hard to feminize'. In his bestselling book *Degeneration*, the Zionist critic Max Nordau amplified, more than a century before Peterson, the fear that the empires and nations of the West are populated by the weak-willed, the effeminate and the degenerate. The French philosopher Georges Sorel identified myth as the necessary antidote to decadence and spur to rejuvenation. An intellectual inspiration to fascists across

Europe, Sorel was particularly nostalgic about the patriarchal systems of ancient Israel and Greece.

Like Peterson, many of these hyper-masculinist thinkers saw compassion as a vice and urged insecure men to harden their hearts against the weak (women and minorities) on the grounds that the latter were biologically and culturally inferior. Hailing myth and dreams as the repository of fundamental human truths, they became popular because they addressed a widely felt spiritual hunger: of men looking desperately for maps of meaning in a world they found opaque and uncontrollable.

It was against this (eerily familiar) background – a 'revolt against the modern world', as the title of Evola's 1934 book put it – that demagogues emerged so quickly in twentieth-century Europe and managed to exalt national and racial myths as the true source of individual and collective health. The drastic individual makeover demanded by the visionaries turned out to require a mass, coerced retreat from failed liberal modernity into an idealised traditional realm of myth and ritual.

In the end, deskbound pedants and fantasists helped bring about, in Thomas Mann's words in 1936, an extensive 'moral devastation' with their 'worship of the unconscious' – that 'knows no values, no good or evil, no morality'. Nothing less than the foundations for knowledge and ethics, politics and science, collapsed, ultimately triggering the cataclysms of the twentieth century: two world wars, totalitarian regimes and the Holocaust. It is no exaggeration to say that we are in the midst of a similar intellectual and moral breakdown, one that seems to presage a great calamity. Peterson calls it, correctly, 'psychological and social dissolution'. But he is a disturbing symptom of the malaise to which he promises a cure.

2018

10

What Is Great About Ourselves

On Salvaging Liberalism

Is it finally closing time in the gardens of the West? The wails that have rent the air since the Brexit vote and Trump's victory rise from the same parts of Anglo-America that hosted, post-1989, the noisiest celebrations of liberalism, democracy, free markets and globalisation. Bill Emmott, the former editor of the *Economist*, writes that 'the fear now is of being present at the destruction' of the 'West', the 'world's most successful political idea'. Edward Luce, for example, a *Financial Times* columnist based in Washington, DC, isn't sure 'whether the Western way of life, and our liberal democratic systems, can survive'. Donald Trump has also chimed in, asking 'whether the West has the will to survive'. These apocalyptic Westernists long to turn things around, to make their shattered world whole again. David Goodhart, the founding editor of *Prospect*, told the *New York Times* just before the general election that he believed Theresa May could dominate British politics for a generation. Mark Lilla, a professor at Columbia and a regular contributor to the *New York Review of Books*, wants the Democratic Party, which under Bill Clinton captured 'Americans' imaginations about our shared destiny', to abandon identity politics and help liberalism become once more a 'unifying force' for the 'common good'. Douglas Murray, associate editor of the *Spectator*, thinks that Trump might just save Western civilisation.

The ideas and commitments of the new prophets of decline do not emerge from any personal experience of it, let alone adversity of the kind suffered by many voters of Brexit and Trump. These men were ideologically formed during the reign of Reagan and Thatcher, and their influence and prestige have grown in step with the expansion of Anglo-America's intellectual and cultural capital. Lilla, a self-declared 'centrist liberal', arrived at his present position by way of working-class Detroit, evangelical Christianity and an early flirtation with neoconservatism. The British writers belong to a traditional elite; shared privilege transcends ideological discrepancies between centrist liberalism and nativism, the *Financial Times* and the *Spectator*. Murray and Goodhart were educated at Eton; the fathers of both Luce and Goodhart were Conservative MPs. Inhabitants of a trans-atlantic ecosystem of corporate philanthropy, think tanks and high-altitude conclaves, they can also be found backslapping in the review pages and on Twitter: Murray calls Goodhart's writing 'superb' and Luce's 'beautiful'; Emmott thanks Murray for his 'nice' review in *The Times*.

Goodhart is an especially interesting case. A former jour-nalist on the *Financial Times*, he founded *Prospect* in 1995 together with Derek Coombs, a former Conservative MP and wealthy businessman (subsequently part-owned by a hedge fund, *Prospect*'s current majority shareholder is a financial investment firm in the City). Avowedly 'centre-left' when the centre seemed the right place to be, *Prospect* exemplified the alliance between finance, business and New Labour. In no other mainstream periodical was the prospectus for New Labour's blend of social and economic liberalism so clearly stated. Blair himself argued there for the 'Third Way' and the imperatives of 'modernisation'. In August 2002, a few months after Blair became a proselytiser for Bush's global war on terror, Goodhart wrote that Blair had 'reshaped British politics, if not yet Britain, and is Europe's heaviest hitter. He knows what he is up to and has the intellectual confidence to describe it.'

A year later, however, Goodhart felt that 'Tony Blair has finally lost his Midas touch.' In October 2004, he carried the first of a long series of eulogies to Gordon Brown, then 'odds-on to be prime minister before the end of 2008'. 'The Brown transition', Goodhart wrote, 'could help to realise the centre-left's dream of governing Britain for a generation.' What had happened?

Nothing had shaken Goodhart's faith in neo-liberalism: he was marvelling in 2005, two years before the worst financial crisis in history, that economics had ceased 'to dominate political debate'. He did feel, however, that a third-term Labour government was 'struggling to fashion an appropriate response to the new salience of security and identity issues'. Goodhart himself had prioritised issues of ethnic and racial identity over the perennially salient problems of class and gender in a *Prospect* article titled 'Too Diverse?' 'We not only live among stranger citizens . . . squashed together on buses, trains and tubes,' he observed, 'but we must share with them.' Elsewhere, he has argued that 'most of us prefer our own kind' and that immigration is undermining social solidarity and traditional identities, eroding Britain's 'common culture' and making it 'increasingly full of mysterious and unfamiliar worlds'. Elites supporting 'separatist' multiculturalism, he wrote, had 'privileged minority identities over common citizenship'. Consequently, they had drifted out of touch with the views of ordinary people.

Goodhart getting down with the common people was a curious sight. He seemed aware of this, continually presenting himself as a brave contrarian, resisting a tenacious metropolitan consensus that was in favour of immigration and multiculturalism. 'I am now post-liberal and proud,' Goodhart wrote in March, and his new book proposes that the main political fault line in British society is the one dividing a powerful minority of university-educated professional 'Anywheres' (people like Goodhart) from disempowered 'Somewheres', who have 'rooted' identities based in 'group belonging and particular places'.

Anywheres prize 'autonomy, mobility and novelty' over 'group identity, tradition and national social contracts'. 'Somewheres', who are 'socially conservative and communitarian by instinct', resist immigration and diversity.

In affiliating himself with the Somewheres, who in his view constitute the majority of the British population, Goodhart seems more majoritarian than contrarian. At last year's Conservative Party conference, Theresa May reproved 'citizens of nowhere' for their rootless cosmopolitanism. Moreover, the straw-manning of multiculturalism has been popular in Britain's right-wing press since Khomeini's fatwa against Salman Rushdie. And there is nothing 'post-liberal' about arguments for a less diverse population. Liberalism, flatteringly identified by Goodhart with cosmopolitan tolerance, has long been more at home with nationalism, imperialism and even racialism. Scholars from Uday S. Mehta to Duncan Bell have demonstrated that nineteenth-century liberal prescriptions about freedom and progress, emerging in an age of imperial expansion and capitalist globalisation, presupposed a chasm between civilised whites and uncivilised non-whites. Victorian liberals from Mill to Hobhouse simply assumed ethnic homogeneity at home and racial hierarchy abroad.

It was the historic reversal of population movements between the colonies and the metropolis after 1945 that incited a new 'racism without races' and 'anti-Semitism without Jews' (Gunther Anders's phrase for the treatment of Turkish guest workers in post-war Germany). In Britain, a bipartisan prejudice governed the subject of 'race relations' long after *Windrush*. Many former imperialists, such as Enoch Powell, had never stopped thinking in the categories mandated by their previously unchallenged dominance. In 1968, Powell warned that immigration from Britain's former colonies would lead to a dire situation in which 'the black man will have the whip hand over the white man'; ten years later, prime minister-in-waiting Margaret Thatcher claimed in a television interview that British people were 'really rather afraid that this country might be rather swamped by people with a different culture'.

A moral panic about people with a different culture is central to Goodhart's world view. The same panic drove the growth of far-right movements across Western Europe in the 1980s. The Front National (FN) in particular advanced the right to be culturally distinctive, and to exclude outsiders who would radically transform white, Christian Europe. In this vision, cultures rather than biologically defined races were presented as exclusive and unchanging across time and place, with cultural difference treated as a fact of nature – 'rooted' identities, in Goodhart's phrase – that we ignore at our peril. Preferring our own kind, we apparently belong, in defiance of human history, to an immutable community bound by its origins to a specific place, and should have the right to remain distinctive.

Busily naturalising cultural difference, the neo-anthropologists were careful not to preen about their superior origins and heredity as the supremacists of the past had done. They could even claim to be aficionados of racial diversity. 'I love Maghrebins,' Jean-Marie Le Pen declared, 'but their place is in the Maghreb.' Similarly, Goodhart earnestly regrets racism as an inevitable consequence of ignoring the natural and insurmountable divisions between people. From this perspective, liberal multiculturalists and leftists are the ones enabling racism, by ignoring the psychological and sociological repercussions of squashing ineluctably dissimilar people together on buses, trains and tubes.

Goodhart makes no attempt to figure out why a moral panic about people with a different culture has emerged against a background of obscene inequalities, progressive deregulation of labour markets and a massive expansion in the ranks of the precariat. He is indifferent, too, to the changes in working-class life and immigration patterns since 1945. Post-war immigrants from Britain's former colonies arrived in a country enjoying full employment, a growing welfare state and potent working-class politics. Recent immigrants land in a country whose manufacturing base has crumbled, whose welfare state is weakened and whose trade unions are neutered.

New Labour's surrender to the Thatcherite creed that 'there is no alternative' ruled out the party's commitments to welfare-state social democracy and nationalisation. How, then, would it reconcile privatisation, worship of the entrepreneur and a general state of relaxation about people getting filthy rich with Labour's old base in the public-sector middle class and working class?

In *Free World: Why a Crisis of the West Reveals the Opportunity of Our Times*, an early dirge about the waning of Anglo-American power, Timothy Garton Ash approvingly quoted a Canadian friend as saying that the trouble with Britain is that 'it doesn't know what story it wants to tell.' This was undoubtedly true of New Labour, which had invested heavily in storytelling and spin as substitutes for substantive change. Its projection of 'Cool Britannia' failed. The popular culture it referred to, as Stuart Hall pointed out, was 'too "multicultural" and too "Black British" or "Asian crossover" or "British hybrid" for New Labour's more sober, corporate-managerialist English style'. The only alternative was populist nationalism. In 2010, Gavin Kelly, former deputy chief of staff to Gordon Brown, defined this project in *Prospect*: to complement '"materialism" with a national popular project, embedded in the cultural aspirations and attachments of the British people'.

Brown seemed up to the job when, in a lecture at the British Council in 2004, he appreciatively cited Goodhart along with Melanie Phillips and Roger Scruton in a disquisition on the 'core values of Britishness' ('There is indeed a golden thread that runs through British history of the individual standing firm for freedom and liberty against tyranny'). On a trip to East Africa the following year, he announced that 'the days of Britain having to apologise for its colonial past are over.' No matter that Britain had never apologised: like his fellow Scot Niall Ferguson, Brown wanted British people to feel proud of their empire. At a conference in 2006 on 'the future of Britishness', Brown outlined an American-style patriotism, provoking even David Cameron, newly appointed as Tory leader, to object, 'We're not like that. We don't do flags.' Meanwhile, at *Prospect*, Goodhart was thrilled that 'the national agenda is focusing on duty, community and stability . . . the "respect" legislation, school discipline, ID cards, identity and Britishness.' When Brown finally moved into Downing Street in 2007, *Prospect* celebrated with a cover proclaiming 'Gordon Brown, Intellectual'.

Goodhart's romance with Brown, and with intellectualism in general, eventually soured, to the extent that he began to root for the 'dowdy' and 'inarticulate' Theresa May, on the grounds that 'we've done enough admiring of the cognitive elites and their marvellous articulacy.' As early as 2008, sensing 'drift and decay' in Brown's regime, Goodhart began to navigate the short distance from the centre-left to the reactionary right. In 2009, he hailed the neocon writer Christopher Caldwell, who had claimed that Muslims are 'conquering Europe's cities, street by street', as a brilliant seer, who understood the consequences of undermining 'national tradition' with 'liberal universalism'.

It may be unfair to pick on Goodhart's exertions on behalf of a national popular project. The British press has consistently invited voters to see their struggles through the prism of immigration and dodgy foreigners in general. The upshot has been a rapid pin-striping of bigotry. Cameron's description of refugees as a 'swarm' and fellow Etonians Zac Goldsmith and Boris Johnson's calling London's Muslim mayor a 'terrorist sympathiser' are of a part with Katie Hopkins's comparison of migrants to 'cockroaches' and a deranged man's shout of 'Britain First' as he assassinated a member of Parliament.

But Goodhart's acute discomfort with diversity also reflects the profound fears and insecurities felt by metropolitan intellectuals in the second phase of globalisation. The events of 9/11, and then a series of humiliating debacles in the war on terror, cracked the illusion of superiority and security shared by Western writers and journalists during the Cold War and the euphoric decade that followed its end. The unexpected rise of China in the 2000s aggravated the post-imperial anxiety that, to borrow Sartre's phrase, the West was 'springing leaks everywhere'. The revolt of the insecure intellectuals presaged the revolt of the uprooted masses. Writing in the *Financial Times* in 2006, Lionel Shriver confessed to feeling pushed out by Guatemalan immigrants who had 'colonised' a recreation area in New York's Riverside Park ('The last few times I practised my forehand, I drew wary looks and felt unwelcome'). Asserting that the 'full-scale invasion of the first world by the third has begun', Shriver anticipated the Brexiteers' comparison of immigration to Nazism. 'Britain', she wrote, 'memorialises its natives' brave fight against the Nazis in the Second World War.' But 'the arrival of foreign populations can begin to duplicate the experience of military occupation – your nation is no longer your home'.

Shriver's reference to plucky British 'natives' excluded the millions of Indians and African soldiers in the imperial army who fought Britain's enemies across three continents. But then oppositions between 'us' and 'them', natives and foreigners, cannot be forged without suppressing the history of imperialism, which coerced all human beings into a single, cruelly stratified space, turning a vast majority into permanent losers. The long-term winners, now encouraged to check their privilege, can't claim victimhood without obscuring the fact that conquest and colonisation endowed them with disproportionate wealth, power and intellectual authority. Unnerved by the prospect of decline, some members of this exalted minority began to conflate their own relative diminution with a more general disintegration, and to cultivate a dread of uppity minorities. Their paranoid conspiracies entered the mainstream long before anyone had heard of Breitbart News or Steve Bannon. The Canadian journalist Mark Steyn, who hoped in *America Alone: The End of the World as We Know It* that all Europeans would eventually come to the same conclusion that the Serbs had – 'If you can't outbreed the enemy, cull 'em' – was hailed by Martin Amis as a 'great sayer of the unsayable'. Bruce Bawer's *While Europe Slept: How Radical Islam Is Destroying the West from Within* was nominated for the National Book Critics Circle award, prompting one judge, Eliot Weinberger, to denounce Bawer for engaging in 'racism as criticism'.

Worried that Hispanics were undermining 'Anglo-Protestant society', Samuel Huntington, writing in *Who Are We? The Challenges to America's National Identity*, denounced multiculturalism as an anti-Western ideology. Westerners themselves, others argued, were the most fanatical anti-Westernists. On this view, a tradition of critical self-reflection, created to make sense of the atrocities of imperialism, slavery, genocide and two world wars, had trapped Westerners in self-loathing. As Pascal Bruckner put it in *The Tyranny of Guilt: An Essay on Western Masochism*, 'Nothing is more Western than hatred of the West.' In 2011, Anders Behring Breivik reproduced many of these arguments against 'cultural Marxists' and liberal multiculturalists in the 1,500-page manifesto he wrote before killing dozens of children at a Social Democrat youth camp in Norway.

'The intelligentsia, once the vanguard of the ascending bourgeoisie, becomes the lumpen-bourgeoisie in the age of its decay,' Arthur Koestler wrote. Nowhere in Anglo-America is this phenomenon more evident than in the British media, which even at its most reactionary used to maintain some commitment to wit and style. The *Spectator*, once suavely edited, now serves as a fraternity house for Douglas Murray, Toby Young, James Delingpole and Rod Liddle; pummelling Muslims and high-fiving on Brexit, these right-wing bros are to the posh periodicals what Jeremy Clarkson was to the BBC.

Murray's book-length screed, *The Strange Death of Europe*, is full of Trump-style imaginings of uncontrollable Muslims killing and raping their way across a hapless continent. In an earlier book, *Neoconservatism: Why We Need It*, he explained that American neocons possess a 'moral clarity' that allows them to find 'answers to many of the problems facing America and the world today'. Murray defended the invasion of Iraq and proposed some American remedies for Britain's ailing 'socialist' economy ('Slash taxes . . . public services should be cut, and again not just cut, but slashed'). Murray's latest offering is an unlikely lament, coming from a gay atheist, for the death of Christianity and the loss of Europe's ancient cultural unity. A blurb from Roger Scruton graces the back cover, and the lessons of the master are evident in Murray's investigation of popular culture ('Unbearable shallowness. Was the sum of European endeavour and achievement really meant to culminate in this?'). He finds some figures to praise, like Hungary's Viktor Orbán, who is intrepidly trying to keep Europe Christian by keeping Muslims out, and members of Pegida and the English Defence League, who are viciously defamed by politicians and journalists for making perfectly reasonable points. Recent events in the United States have also given Murray hope. In July he praised 'the leader of the free world' for 'reminding the West of what is great about ourselves and giving an unapologetic defence of that greatness'.

Edward Luce, a former speechwriter for the former US Treasury Secretary Larry Summers, has few illusions today about the Washington consensus he once helped promote: 'Countries that swallowed the prescription suffered terribly.' Social mobility is a delusion: 'The meritocratic society has given way to a hereditary meritocracy.' 'Western liberal democracy is not yet dead,' he writes, 'but it is far closer to collapse than we may wish to believe.' His apostasies risk alienating many in his post–Cold War generation of Anglo-American commentators whom the advent of Trump has thrown into despair, and who feel nostalgia for the good old days of the 'liberal order'. As Fareed Zakaria wrote in a nervous review of *The Retreat of Western Liberalism* in the *New York Times*, 'We all deserve criticism for missing the phenomenon of the "left-behinds",' but 'there remain powerful reasons to embrace and uphold the liberal international order.' 'In France,' for instance, 'Macron is articulating a defence of Western democracy.'

As it happens, Luce is a more resolute liberal internationalist than Zakaria in his belief that Modi's India would defend Western democracy better than any Western country would. Evidently, Luce cannot entirely break free from the ideological formation of his social and professional set. 'Washington backed would-be democrats across the world during the Cold War,' he wrote in a recent column. This is a neat reversal of the facts.

Luce admires Lilla's 'impeccable liberal credentials', and quotes his admonition in a *New York Times* op-ed that 'liberals should bear in mind that the first identity movement in American politics was the Ku Klux Klan, which still exists. Those who play the identity game should be prepared to lose it.' Neither Luce nor Lilla thinks to mention that powerful white men were playing the identity game more than a century before the Ku Klux Klan was founded, or that racial exclusion has long been central to liberal universalism. Lilla, who praised the founding fathers' 'achievement in establishing a system of government based on the guarantee of rights', continues to offer in his new book the view from Mount Rushmore (and Paris, where, as an intellectual historian of France, he seems to have cultivated his peculiarly colour-blind notion of equal citizenship). French and American republics that promised democratic rights to all enforced at the same time a global hierarchy in which those rights were reserved for some and forbidden to the rest. America's own exponents of self-evident truths withheld equal rights from women, and inflicted slavery on blacks and extermination on Native Americans. The long-postponed end of segregation in the 1960s actually made exclusionary identity politics central to American democracy. Nixon's Southern Strategy and Reagan's war on drugs successfully stoked majoritarian fears of dark-skinned minorities. In describing Hispanic and Muslim immigrants as existential threats to the US, Trump was playing a game whose rules the founding fathers had laid down: making racial degradation the basis of solidarity among property-owning white men.

Lilla has little time for the historic victims of a majority's potent identity politics. According to him, Black Lives Matter, with its 'Mau Mau tactics', is 'a textbook example of how not to build solidarity'. 'We need no more marchers,' he declares, or 'social justice warriors'. Instead we need 'more mayors' and politicians able to imagine, as Reagan and Clinton apparently did, a 'common good'. Lilla also repeats his earlier claim that the dupes of cultural studies and multiculturalism on university campuses are primarily to blame for Trump rather than his election being a consequence of the catastrophic loss of jobs, pensions, homes and self-esteem. Lilla says he is 'appalled' by an 'ideology institutionalised in colleges and universities that fetishises our individual and group attachments, applauds self-absorption and casts a shadow of suspicion over any application of a universal democratic "we"'.

Extensive economic distress in Lilla's account seems a secondary phenomenon to Rhodes Must Fall, and minority agitators asking for an end to historical injustice appear to be needlessly provoking and alienating an honest majority constituted by the white working classes or rooted Somewheres. His phrase 'social justice warriors' mocks the struggles for recognition and dignity on the part of people who have suffered not only from the barefaced identity politics of the right but also from the equivocations of the 'white moderate' – once identified by Martin Luther King as a bigger obstacle than the 'Ku Klux Klanner'. But it is Lilla's contemptuous reference to 'Mau Mau tactics' that confirms the suspicion that an Anglo-American intelligentsia, confronted by the political and intellectual assertiveness of previously silent or invisible minorities and frustrated by its apparent failure to take back control, was the vanguard of the Brexiteers and the Trumpists. Certainly, to read *The*

Once and Future Liberal is to understand why the cries of 'check your privilege' from the descendants of slaves grow louder all the time.

Lilla's critique of minority-ism appeared just as Trump successfully remobilised white majoritarianism. Spectacularly ill-timed, it was nevertheless keenly embraced by the vital centrists, who cannot resist blaming Anglo-America's political calamities on the pampering of minorities. 'Trump and his supporters', Simon Jenkins wrote in the *Guardian* after the white supremacist march in Charlottesville, 'thrive on the venom of their liberal tormentors.' Perhaps such back-to-front conclusions are inevitable if the centrist establishment stays silent about its own iniquities and failures. Beating up cultural Marxists and identity liberals may even be mandatory if you believe that Reagan and Clinton, two hectic jailers of African Americans and slashers of social security, were promoters of the common good, and if your deepest wish is for figures like Brown and May to dominate politics for a generation.

'Most of the white people I have ever known', James Baldwin once wrote, 'impressed me as being in the grip of a weird nostalgia, dreaming of a vanished state of security and order.' Today, longing for the *ancien régime* increasingly defines the Atlantic seaboard's pundits as much as it does the fine people defending the honour of Robert E. Lee. It remains to be seen whether America, Britain, Europe and liberalism can be made great again. But it already seems clear that the racial supremacist in the White House and many of his opponents are engaged in the same endeavour: to extend closing time in their own gardens in the West.

2017

11

Why Do White People
Like What I Write?

On Ta-Nehisi Coates

During the big anti-war protests in early 2003, Ta-Nehisi Coates was a deliveryman for a deli in Park Slope, Brooklyn. He, too, was 'sceptical', he wrote a decade later in a blog post for the *Atlantic*, 'but if the US was going to take out a mad tyrant, who was I to object?' After all, as Coates remembered, 'every "sensible" and "serious" person you knew – left or right – was for the war.' 'I am not a radical,' Coates said. Even so he found it 'searing' to watch 'reasonable people assemble sober arguments for a disaster'.

In retrospect, the most remarkable of these reasonable people were not the neoconservatives but the liberals – some of them now Coates's colleagues and supporters – who recommended war and condoned torture while advancing America's mission to bring democracy to the world's benighted. In *The Fight Is for Democracy*, George Packer argued that a 'vibrant, hardheaded liberalism' could use the American military to promote its values. The subtitle of *The Good Fight* by Peter Beinart, then the editor of the *New Republic*, insisted 'Why Liberals – and Only Liberals – Can Win the War on Terror and Make America Great Again.' 'It's time to think of torture,' *Newsweek* declared a few weeks after 9/11. 'Focused brutality', *Time* recommended. *Vanity Fair* praised Rumsfeld for his 'oddly reassuring ruthlessness'. As the invasion of Iraq got under way, the *Atlantic*, described as 'prestigious' by Coates in his new book, walked its readers through the advantages of 'torture-lite' in a cover story. In the *New York Times Magazine*, Michael Ignatieff, biographer of Isaiah Berlin and professor of human rights, exhorted Americans to embrace their imperial destiny and offered his own suggestions for 'permissible duress'. Even the *New Yorker*, fastidiously aloof from Beltway schemers during the Cold War, published a report by Jeffrey Goldberg, the *Atlantic*'s current editor, detailing links between al-Qaida and Iraq – links later revealed to be non-existent.

Goldberg's article was seized on by Bush and Cheney: the *New Yorker* had become, as an unusually bold writer in the *Nation* pointed out, 'one more courtier straining to get the king's ear'. But the Bush administration didn't need eggheads to euphemise pre-emptive war, torture, rendition and indefinite offshore detention. Bush's own demotic – 'We'll smoke them out', 'wanted dead or alive', 'Pretty soon, we'll have to start displaying scalps' – repeatedly invoked wars of extirpation against what the Declaration of Independence had called 'merciless Indian Savages'. 'When this is all over,' Cofer Black, Bush's chief counterterrorist adviser, assured his boss, 'the bad guys are going to have flies walking across their eyeballs.' The mood was infectious among the personnel in charge of exterminating the brutes. The *Atlantic*'s Robert Kaplan cheerfully reported that 'Welcome to Injun Country' was the refrain among American soldiers worldwide. The primal bloodlusts of the war on terror survived Obama's renaming of it. The Seal team that in 2011 eventually scalped Osama bin Laden (code-named Geronimo) carried fourteen-inch hatchets made by a North Carolina knife-maker known for his blades in the 1992 film *The Last of the Mohicans*. Obama administration officials volunteered details of the wildly popular slaying to the makers of the 2012 film *Zero Dark Thirty*, which depicted (falsely) swarthy villains revealing bin Laden's hideout under torture.

~

'A racist society can't but fight a racist war,' James Baldwin wrote in 1967; 'the assumptions acted on at home are also acted on abroad.' During the war on terror the traffic between the US and various shithole countries wasn't only in assumptions: there was also a wholesale exporting of equipment, technologies of torture and bad lieutenants. To take one instance, Richard Zuley, a specialist at Guantánamo, had become reassuringly ruthless while working for a Chicago police unit that for decades inter-rogated predominantly African Americans at so-called black sites. It's only now, with a white supremacist ensconced in the White House, that those same hardheaded liberals – who did so much to create a climate of opinion and a legal regime in which black and brown bodies could be seized, broken and destroyed outside all norms and laws of war – are coming to grips with 'America's Original Sin: Slavery and the Legacy of White Supremacy' (an unlikely recent headline in *Foreign Affairs*). Back in the early 2000s the liberal universalists seemed unaware that their project might be fatally flawed, and that America's own democracy had been secured by mass bondage, colonial dispossession and wars of aggression; they still hadn't fully reckoned with the historical legacy of institutionalised racial cruelty, inequality and division – what Coates has come to describe.

'In America,' Coates writes, 'it is traditional to destroy the black body – it is heritage.' 'To be black' is to be perpetually 'naked before the elements of the world, before all the guns, fists, knives, crack, rape, and disease'. The liberal freedoms of propertied men were always defined against omnipresent threats: mutinous natives, rebellious slaves. The white man, Tocqueville wrote as he observed race relations in America, 'is to the men of other races what man himself is to the animals', in the sense that he 'makes them serve his purposes, and when he cannot make them bend, he destroys them'. A social order built on systemic violence made the black man, Tocqueville recog-nised, an ever-present menace in his white master's imagination.

This proximity to a nemesis made a culture of fear central to American politics, entailing a continuous investment in the machinery of coercion, surveillance and control, along with pre-emptive brutality against internal and external enemies.

Coates, who was born in 1975, came of age just as a new Jim Crow was emerging domestically to accompany Bush Sr's new world order. 'By God, we've kicked the Vietnam Syndrome once and for all!' So Bush Sr said in a euphoric victory statement at the end of the Gulf War. The kicking of the Vietnam Syndrome and 'Saddam Hussein's ass' signalled the removal of all restraints on American power imposed by dogged gooks and their traitorous allies on the American left. With America free to police the world, old legal and moral barriers were also dismantled at home. Just as Coates entered Howard University and began his harsh education in American history, the stage was set for a pitiless imposition of market discipline and evisceration of welfare-state protections. Such drastic socio-economic re-engineering required a fresh public consensus, and a racialised view of crime and national security came in handy in separating the deserving from the undeserving. Under Reagan, the police had started to resemble the military with its special weapons and bellicose posturing. The prison–industrial complex burgeoned under Bill Clinton: an incarcerated population of 300,000 in 1970 expanded to 2.1 million in 2000 – the majority black and brown, and poor. Liberals did not simply inherit Republican schemes of harsh policing and extreme punishment. They took the initiative. Clinton, hailed as the 'first black president' by Toni Morrison, ended what he called 'welfare as we know it' and deregulated financial markets. Amid a national panic about 'street terrorists', he signed the most draconian crime bill in US history in 1994, following it up two years later with an anti-terrorism bill that laid the foundation for the Patriot Act of 2001.

The intimate relationship between America's internal and external wars, established by its original sin, has long been clear.

The question was always how long mainstream intellectuals could continue to offer fig-leaf euphemisms for shock-and-awe racism, and suppress an entwined history of white supremacism and militarisation with fables about American exceptionalism, liberalism's long battle with totalitarianism, and that sort of thing. Hurricane Katrina, coming after the non-discovery of WMDs in Iraq, undermined liberal faith in Bush's heavily racialised war. American claims to global moral leadership since the 1960s had depended greatly on the apparent breakthrough of the civil rights movement, and the sidelining of the bigots who screamed 'Segregation now, segregation tomorrow, segregation for ever'. In New Orleans, black bodies naked before the elements of the world – elements which included trigger-happy Blackwater mercenaries guarding the rich – made it clear that old-style racial separation had been replaced by sharply defined zones of prosperity and destitution: segregation for ever. But the apparent successes of social liberalism, culminating in Obama's election, managed to obscure the new regimes of racial sequester for a while longer. Since the 1990s, the bonanzas of free trade and financial deregulation had helped breed greater tolerance for racial and sexual variety, primarily among the privileged – the CIA under Obama set up a recruiting office at the Miami Beach Gay Pride parade. Overt racism and homophobia had become taboo, even as imprisonment or premature death removed 1.5 million black men from public life. Diversification and multiculturalism among upwardly mobile, college-educated elites went together with mass incarceration at home and endless military interventions abroad.

In many ways, Coates's career manifests these collateral trends of progress and regress in American society. He grew up in Baltimore at the height of the crack epidemic. One of his own friends at Howard University in the 1990s was murdered by the police. Coates didn't finish college and had been working and writing for small magazines when in 2008 he was commissioned by the *Atlantic* to write a blog during Obama's campaign for president. Three books and many blog posts and tweets later, Coates is, in Packer's words, 'the most influential writer in America today' – an elevation that no writer of colour could previously have achieved. Toni Morrison claims he has filled 'the intellectual void that plagued me after James Baldwin died'. Philip Roth has been led to histories of American racism by Coates's books. David Brooks credits him for advancing an 'education for white people' that evidently began after 'Ferguson, Baltimore, Charleston and the other killings'. Even *USA Today* thinks that 'to have such a voice, in such a moment, is a ray of light.'

Coates seems genuinely embarrassed by his swift celebrity: by the fact that, as he writes in his latest book, *We Were Eight Years in Power*, a collection of essays published in the *Atlantic* between 2008 and 2016, 'I, who'd begun in failure, who held no degrees or credentials, had become such a person.' He also visibly struggles with the question, 'Why do white people like what I write?' This is a fraught issue for the very few writers from formerly colonised countries or historically disadvantaged minorities in the West who are embraced by 'legacy' periodicals, and then tasked with representing their people – or country, religion, race, and even continent (as in the *New York Times*'s praise for Salman Rushdie: 'A continent finding its voice'). Relations between the anointed 'representative' writer and those who are denied this privilege by white gatekeepers are notoriously prickly. Coates, a self-made writer, is particularly vulnerable to the charge that he is popular among white liberals since he assuages their guilt about racism.

He did not have until recently a perch in academia, where most prominent African-American intellectuals have found a stable home. Nor is he affiliated to any political movement – he is sceptical of the possibilities of political change – and, unlike his bitter critic, Cornel West, he is an atheist. Identified solely with the *Atlantic*, a periodical better known for its oligarchic shindigs than its subversive content, Coates also seems distant from the tradition of black magazines like *Reconstruction*, *Transition* and *Emerge*, or left-wing journals like *n+1*, *Dissent* and *Jacobin*. He credits his large white fan club to Obama. Fascination with a black president, he thinks, 'eventually expanded into curiosity about the community he had so consciously made his home and all the old, fitfully slumbering questions he'd awakened about American identity'. This is true, but only in the way a banality is true. Most mainstream publications have indeed tried in recent years to accommodate more writers and journalists from racial and ethnic minorities. But the relevant point, perhaps impolitic for Coates to make, is that those who were assembling sensible arguments for war and torture in prestigious magazines only a few years ago have been forced to confront, along with their readers, the obdurate pathologies of American life that stem from America's original sin.

Coates, followed by the 'white working classes', has surfaced into liberal consciousness during the pained if still very partial self-reckoning among American elites that began with Hurricane Katrina. Many journalists have been scrambling, more feverishly since Trump's apotheosis, to account for the stunningly extensive experience of fear and humiliation across racial and gender divisions; some have tried to reinvent themselves in heroic resistance to Trump and authoritarian 'populism'. David Frum, geometer under George W. Bush of an intercontinental 'axis of evil', now locates evil in the White House. Max Boot, self-declared 'neo-imperialist' and exponent of 'savage wars', recently claimed to have become aware of his 'white privilege'. Ignatieff, advocate of empire-lite and torture-lite, is presently embattled on behalf of the open society in Mitteleuropa. Goldberg, previously known as stenographer to Netanyahu, is now Coates's diligent promoter. Amid this brisk laundering of reputations, and a turnover of 'woke' white men, Coates has seized the opportunity to describe American power from the rare standpoint of its internal victims.

As a self-professed autodidact, Coates is primarily concerned to share with readers his most recent readings and discoveries. His essays are milestones in an accelerated self-education, with Coates constantly summoning himself to fresh modes of thinking. Very little in his book will be unfamiliar to readers of histories of American slavery and the mounting scholarship on the new Jim Crow. Coates, who claimed in 2013 to be 'not a radical', now says he has been 'radicalised', and as a black writer in overwhelmingly white media, he has laid out the varied social practices of racial discrimination with estimable power and skill. But the essays in *We Were Eight Years in Power*, so recent and so much discussed on their first publication, already feel like artefacts of a moribund social liberalism. Reparations for slavery may have seemed 'the indispensable tool against white supremacy' when Obama was in power. It is hard to see how this tool can be deployed against Trump. The documentation in Coates's essays is consistently impressive, especially in his writing about mass imprisonment and housing discrimination. But the chain of causality that can trace the complex process of exclusion in America to its grisly consequences – the election of a racist and serial groper – is missing from his book. Nor can we understand from his account of self-radicalisation why the words 'socialism' and 'imperialism' became meaningful to a young generation of Americans during what he calls 'the most incredible of eras – the era of a black president'. There is a conspicuous analytical lacuna here, and it results from an overestimation, increasingly commonplace in the era of Trump, of the most incredible of eras, and an underestimation of its continuities with the past and present.

In the sentimental education of Coates, and of many liberal intellectuals mugged by American realities, Obama is the culmination of the civil rights movement, the figure who fulfils the legacies of Malcolm X as well as Martin Luther King. In Jay Z's words, 'Rosa sat so Martin could walk; Martin walked so Obama could run; Obama is running so we all can fly!' John

McCain, hapless Republican candidate in 2008, charged that his rival was a lightweight international 'celebrity', like Britney Spears. To many white liberals, however, Obama seemed to guarantee instant redemption from the crimes of a democracy built on slavery and genocide. There is no doubt that compared to the 'first black president', who played the dog whistle better than the saxophone, a hip hop enthusiast and the son of a Kenyan Muslim represented a genuine diversification of America's ruling class. Obama offered his own ascent as proof that America is an inclusive society, ceaselessly moving towards a 'more perfect union'. But such apparent vindications of the American dream obscured the limited achievement of the civil rights movement, and the fragility of the social and political consensus behind it. The widespread belief that Obama had inaugurated a 'post-racial' age helped conceal the ways in which the barefaced cruelties of segregation's distant past had been softening since the 1960s into subtle exclusions and injustices.

A ruling class that had been forced to make partial concessions to the civil rights movement subsequently worked, as Nixon blurted out, to 'devise a system' to deal with the black 'problem' without appearing to do so. With the wars on crime, drugs and welfare queens, the repertoire of deception came to include coded appeals to a white constituency, the supposedly 'silent majority'. But the cruellest trick used by both Republicans and Democrats was the myth that America had resolved the contradiction at the heart of its democracy. For the conviction that African Americans were walking and running and would soon start flying, enabled by equal opportunity, paved the way for an insidious ideological force: colour-blind universalism. Its deceit was summed up best by the creepy Supreme Court justice Antonin Scalia: 'In the eyes of the government, we are just one race here. It is American.' The rules of colour-blind equality and the 'level playing field', as they came to be outlined in the 1980s and 1990s, created a climate in which affirmative action came to look like reverse racism: unacceptably discriminatory against whites. With structural injustice presented as a thing of the past, what appeared to deform the lives of black people was their culture of single-parent households, scant work ethic, criminality and welfare dependency. This widespread attitude was summed up by a *New Republic* cover in 1996 urging Clinton to slash welfare: it showed a black woman, or 'welfare mom', bottle-feeding an infant while smoking. Blacks, in this politically bipartisan view, needed to get with the American programme just as various immigrant communities had done. As the original exponent of centrist liberalism, Arthur Schlesinger Jr, charged, they had become too prone to 'nourishing prejudice, magnifying difference and stirring up antagonism' – in other words, blacks were guilty of identity politics.

The detractors of 'identity liberalism' are still prone to the fantasy that the end of *de jure* racial inequality ushered in a new era of opportunity and mobility for African Americans. In reality, even the black people admitted into the networks of prosperity and privilege remained vulnerable compared to those who had enjoyed the inherited advantages of income and opportunity over several generations. This became gruesomely evident during the financial crisis of 2008, when African-American families, deceived into homeownership by banks peddling subprime loans, found themselves in economic freefall, losing half their collective wealth. When Coates and Obama simultaneously emerged into public view in 2008 the political and ideological foundations of racial progress ought to have looked very shaky. But this structural weakness was obscured by the spectacular upward mobility of an Ivy League-educated black lawyer and constitutional scholar.

There were signs during Obama's campaign, particularly his eagerness to claim the approbation of Henry Kissinger, that he would cruelly disappoint his left-leaning young supporters' hopes of epochal transformation. His actions in office soon made it clear that some version of bait and switch had occurred. Obama had condemned the air war in South Asia as immoral because of its high civilian toll; but three days after his inauguration he ordered drone strikes in Pakistan, and in his first year oversaw more strikes with high civilian casualties than Bush had ordered in his entire presidency. His bellicose speech accepting the Nobel Peace Prize signalled that he would strengthen rather than dismantle the architecture of the open-ended war on terror, while discarding some of its fatuous rhetoric. During his eight years in office, he expanded covert operations and air strikes deep into Africa; girding the continent with American military bases, he exposed large parts of it to violence, anarchy and tyrannical rule. He not only expanded mass surveillance and government data-mining operations at home, and ruthlessly prosecuted whistleblowers, but invested his office with the lethal power to execute anyone, even American citizens, anywhere in the world.

Obama occasionally denounced the 'fat cats' of Wall Street, but Wall Street contributed heavily to his campaign, and he entrusted his economic policy to it early in his tenure, bailing out banks and the insurance mega-company AIG with no quid pro quo. African Americans had turned out in record numbers in 2008, demonstrating their love of an ostensible compatriot, but Obama ensured that he would be immune to the charge of loving blacks too much. Colour-blind to the suffering caused by mortgage foreclosures, he scolded African Americans, using the neo-liberal idiom of individual responsibility, for their moral failings as fathers, husbands and competitors in the global marketplace. Nor did he wish to be seen as soft on immigration; he deported millions of immigrants – Trump is struggling to reach Obama's 2012 peak of 34,000 deportations a month. In his memoir, *Dreams from My Father*, he had eloquently sympathised with the marginalised and the powerless. In power, however, he seemed in thrall to Larry Summers and other members of the East Coast establishment, resembling not so much the permanently alienated outsider as the mixed-race child of imperialism, who, as Ashis Nandy diagnosed in *The Intimate Enemy*, replaces his early feeling for the weak with 'an unending search for masculinity and status'. It isn't surprising that this harbinger of hope and change anointed a foreign-policy hawk and Wall Street-friendly dynast as his heir apparent. His post-presidency moves – kite-surfing with Richard Branson on a private island, extravagantly remunerated speeches to Wall Street and bromance with George Clooney – have confirmed Obama as a case of mistaken identity. As David Remnick, his disappointed biographer, said recently, 'I don't think Obama was immune to lures of the new class of wealth. I think he's very interested in Silicon Valley, stars and showbusiness, and sports, and the rest.'

Embodying neo-liberal chic at its most seductive, Obama managed to restore the self-image of American elites in politics, business and the media that had been much battered during the last years of the Bush presidency. In the updated narrative of American exceptionalism, a black president was instructing the world in the ways of economic and social justice. Journalists in turn helped boost the fantastical promises and unexamined assumptions of universal improvement; some saw Coates himself as an icon of hope and change. A 2015 profile in *New York* magazine describes him at the Aspen Ideas Festival, along with Bill Kristol, Jeffrey Goldberg, assorted plutocrats and their private jets, during the 'late Obama era', when 'progress was in the air' and the 'great question' after the legalisation of gay marriage was, 'would the half-century-long era of increasing prosperity and expanding human freedom prove to be an aberration or a new, permanent state?' Coates is awkward among Aspen's panjandrums. But he thinks it is too easy for him to say he'd be happier in Harlem. 'Truthfully,' he confesses, 'I'm very happy to be here. It's very nice.' According to the profile writer, 'there is a radical chic crowd assembling around Coates' – but then he is 'a writer who radicalises the Establishment'.

For a self-aware and independent-minded writer like Coates, the danger is not so much seduction by power as a distortion of perspective caused by proximity to it. In his account of a party for African-American celebrities at the White House in the late Obama era, his usually majestic syntax withers into *Vanity Fair* puffs: 'Women shivered in their cocktail dresses. Gentlemen chivalrously handed over their suit coats. Naomi Campbell strolled past the security pen in a sleeveless number.' Since Clinton, the reflexive distrust of high office once shared by writers as different as Robert Lowell and Dwight Macdonald has slackened into defensiveness, even adoration, among the American literati. Coates proprietorially notes the ethnic, religious and racial variety of Obama's staff. Everyone seems overwhelmed by a 'feeling', that 'this particular black family, the Obamas, represented the best of black people, the ultimate credit to the race, incomparable in elegance and bearing.' Not so incomparable if you remember Tina Brown's description of another power couple, the Clintons, in the *New Yorker* in 1998: 'Now see your president, tall and absurdly debonair, as he dances with a radiant blonde, his wife.' 'The man in a dinner jacket', Brown wrote, possessed 'more heat than any star in the room (or, for that matter, at the multiplex)'. After his visit, Joe Eszterhas, screenwriter of *Showgirls* and *Basic Instinct*, exulted over the Clinton White House's diverse workforce: 'full of young people, full of women, blacks, gays, Hispanics'. 'Good Lord,' he concluded in *American Rhapsody*, 'we had taken the White House! America was ours.'

A political culture where progress in the air was measured by the president's elegant bearing and penchant for diversity was ripe for demagoguery. The rising disaffection with a narcissistic and callous ruling class was signalled in different ways by the Tea Party, Occupy, Black Lives Matter and Bernie Sanders's insurgent candidacy. The final blow to the Washington (and New York) consensus was delivered by Trump, who correctly read the growing resentment of elites – black or white, meritocratic or dynastic – who presumed to think the White House was theirs. Writing in *Wired* magazine a month before Trump's election, Obama hailed the 'quintessentially American compulsion to race for new frontiers and push the boundaries of what's possible'. Over lunch at the White House, he assured Coates that Trump's victory was impossible. Coates felt 'the same'. He now says that 'adherents and beneficiaries' of white supremacy loathed and feared the black man in the White House – enough to make Trump 'president, and thus put him in position to injure the world'. 'Every white Trump voter is most certainly not a white supremacist,' Coates writes in a bitter epilogue to *We Were Eight Years in Power*. 'But every Trump voter felt it acceptable to hand the fate of the country over to one.' This, again, is true in a banal way, but inadequate as an explanation: Trump also benefited from the disappointment of white voters who had voted, often twice, for Obama, and of black voters who failed to turn out for Hillary Clinton. Moreover, to blame a racist 'whitelash' for Trump is to exculpate the political, business and media luminaries Coates has lately found himself with, especially the journalists disgraced, if not dislodged, by their collaboration in a calamitous racist–imperialist venture to make America great again.

As early as 1935, W.E.B. Du Bois identified fear and loathing of minorities as a 'public and psychological wage' for many whites in American society. More brazenly than his predecessors, Trump linked the misfortunes of the 'white working class' to Chinese cheats, Mexican rapists and treacherous blacks. But racism, Du Bois knew, was not just an ugly or deep-rooted prejudice periodically mobilised by opportunistic politicians and defused by social liberalism: it was a widely legitimated way of ordering social and economic life, with skin colour only one way of creating degrading hierarchies. Convinced that the presumption of inequality and discrimination underpinned the making of the modern world, Du Bois placed his American experience of racial subjection in a broad international context.

Remarkably, all the major black writers and activists of the Atlantic West, from C.L.R. James to Stuart Hall, followed him in this move from the local to the global. Transcending the parochial idioms of their national cultures, they analysed the way in which the processes of capital accumulation and racial domination had become inseparable early in the history of the modern world; the way race emerged as an ideologically flexible category for defining the dangerously lawless civilisational other – black Africans yesterday, Muslims and Hispanics today. The realisation that economic conditions and religion were as much markers of difference as skin colour made Nina Simone, Muhammad Ali and Malcolm X, among others, connect their own aspirations to decolonisation movements in India, Liberia, Ghana, Vietnam, South Africa and Palestine. Martin Luther King absorbed from Gandhi not only the tactic of non-violent protest but also a comprehensive critique of modern imperialism. 'The Black revolution', he argued, much to the dismay of his white liberal supporters, 'is much more than a struggle for the rights of Negroes.'

Compared to these internationalist thinkers, partisans of the second black president, who happen to be the most influential writers and journalists in the US, have provincialised their aspiration for a just society. They have neatly separated it from opposition to an imperial dispensation that incarcerates and deports millions of people each year – disproportionately people of colour – and routinely exercises its right to assault and despoil other countries and murder and torture their citizens. Perceptive about the structural violence of the new Jim Crow, Coates has little to say about its manifestation in the new world order. For all his searing corroboration of racial stigma in America, he has yet to make a connection as vital and powerful as the one that MLK detected in his disillusioned last days between the American devastation of Vietnam and 'the evils that are rooted deeply in the whole structure of our society'. He has so far considered only one of what King identified as 'the giant American triplets of racism, extreme materialism and militarism' – the 'inter-related flaws' that turned American society into a 'burning house' for the blacks trying to integrate into it. And in Coates's world view even race, despite his formidable authority of personal witness, rarely transcends a rancorously polarised American politics of racial division, in which the world's most powerful man appears to have been hounded for eight years by unreconstructed American racists. 'My President Was Black', a 17,000-word profile in the *Atlantic*, is remarkable for its missing interrogations of the black president for his killings by drones; despoliation of Libya, Yemen and Somalia; mass deportations; and cravenness before the titans of finance who ruined millions of black as well as white lives. Coates has been accused of mystifying race and of 'essentialising' whiteness. Nowhere, however, does his view of racial identity seem as static as in his critical tenderness for a black member of the 1 per cent.

As long as Coates is indifferent to the links between race and international political economy, he is more likely to induce relief than guilt among his white liberal fans. They may accept, even embrace, an explanation that blames inveterate bigots in the American heartland for Trump. They would absolutely baulk at the suggestion that the legatee of the civil rights movement upheld a nineteenth-century racist–imperialist order by arrogating to the US presidency the right to kill anyone without due process; they would recoil from the idea that a black man in his eight years in power deepened the juridical legacy of white supremacy before passing it on to a reckless successor. The intractable continuities of institutional brute power should be plain to see. 'The crimes of the American state', Coates writes in one of the introductions to *We Were Eight Years in Power*, 'now had the imprimatur of a black man.' Yet the essays themselves ultimately reveal their author to be safely within the limits of what even a radicalised black man can write in the *Atlantic* without dissolving the rainbow coalition of liberal imperialism or alienating its patrons. Coates's pain and passion have committed him to a long intellectual journey. To move, however, from rage over the rampant destruction of black bodies in America to defensiveness about a purveyor of 'kill lists' in the White House is to cover a very short distance. There is surely more to come. Coates is bracingly aware of his unfinished tasks as a writer. 'Remember that you and I', he writes to his son in *Between the World and Me*, 'are the children of trans-Atlantic rape. Remember the broader consciousness that comes with that. Remember that this consciousness can never ultimately be racial; it must be cosmic.' Nowhere in his published writings has Coates elaborated on what this cosmic consciousness ought to consist of. But his own reference to the slave trade places the black experience at the centre of the modern world: the beginning of a process of capitalism's emergence and globalisation whereby a small minority in Europe and America acquired the awesome power to classify and control almost the entire human population.

The black slave, captured early in this history, presaged the historical ordeal of the millions yet to come: dispossession and brutalisation, the destruction of cultures and memories and of many human possibilities. Today, the practices of kidnapping, predation, extraction, national aggression, mob violence, mass imprisonment, disenfranchisement and zoning pioneered in the Atlantic have travelled everywhere, along with new modes of hierarchy and exclusion. They can be seen in India and Myanmar, where public sanction drives the violent persecution, including lynching, of various internal enemies of the nation. They can be seen in Africa and Latin America. They have returned home to Europe and America as renewed animus against migrants and refugees. All this reproduces to a sinister extent the devastating black experience of fear and danger – of being, as Coates wrote, 'naked before the elements of the world'. Coates's project of unflinching self-education and polemic has never seemed more urgent, and it has only just begun.

2018

12

The Mask It Wears

On Human Rights and Neo-liberalism

American liberals, Samuel Moyn wrote last year in *Dissent*, have never broken 'with the exceptionalist outlook that cast the United States as uniquely virtuous', but having Trump in the 'cockpit of American power' will reveal 'just how terrifyingly normal a nation we are, with our populist jingoism and hawkish foreign policy'. The bipartisan support for the president's bombing campaigns shows that little has changed in this respect, however. As Trump ordered strikes on Syria in April 2017, Fareed Zakaria hailed the 'big moment': 'Donald Trump', he said, 'became president of the United States last night.' As Trump dispatched his 'shiny and new' missiles to Syria a year later, Anne-Marie Slaughter, a former Obama apparatchik and president of the New America Foundation, tweeted that it was the 'right thing' to do. 'It will not stop the war nor save the Syrian people from many other horrors,' Slaughter conceded, and 'it is illegal under international law.' But 'it at least draws a line somewhere & says enough.'

'The deterioration of the intelligentsia', Arthur Koestler wrote, 'is as much a symptom of disease as the corruption of the ruling class or the sleeping sickness of the proletariat. They are symptoms of the same fundamental process.' One clear sign of intellectual infirmity is the desperation with which centrists and liberals, removed from the cockpit of American power, forage for ideas and inspiration on the lumpen right. The *New*

York Times's op-ed page lured Bret Stephens, a climate-change denier, and Bari Weiss, a campus agitator known for persecuting Arab scholars, away from the Murdoch-owned *Wall Street Journal*. The *Atlantic* hired, then a few days later fired, Kevin Williamson, a prose stylist at the *National Review* who suggests that women who have abortions – a quarter of all American women – should be hanged. In this free-for-all, 'thought leaders' rise without a trace, at great speed and with little ballast. Jordan Peterson, a YouTube evangelist who believes that feminists have 'an unconscious wish for brutal male domination', was hailed in the *New York Times* as the West's 'most influential public intellectual' and elicited respectful attention from *New York*, the *Atlantic* and *Esquire*.

The most audacious surfers of the *bien pensant* tide, however, are wealthy and influential stalwarts of the 'liberal order', whose diagnoses and prescriptions dominate the comment pages of the *Financial Times*, the *New York Times* and the *Economist*. They depict the tyro in the White House as an unprecedented calamity, more so evidently than the economic inequality, deadlocked government, subprime debt, offshored jobs, unrestrained corporate power and compromised legislature that made Trump seem a credible candidate to millions of Americans. Hoping to restore their liberal order, journalists, politicians, former civil servants and politically engaged businessmen jostle on both sides of the Atlantic in an air of revivalist zeal. Shortly after Trump's victory, Third Way, a think tank run by a former aide to Bill Clinton, launched New Blue, a $20 million initiative to recharge the vital centre. In April it was revealed that billionaires have been funding Patriots and Pragmatists, a private discussion group of pundits affiliated with the Obama and Bush administrations. In Britain, a centrist political party with a treasure trove of £50 million has surfaced. One of its patrons, Tony Blair, explained in the *New York Times* last March that 'for liberal democracy to survive and thrive, we must build a new coalition that is popular, not populist.' A reinvigorated centrism, he wrote, had to acknowledge 'genuine cultural anxieties', not least on immigration. The same month, Blair laid out £10 million for Renewing the Centre, a 'non-party platform' under the auspices of his Institute for Global Change, and hired Yascha Mounk, a lecturer at Harvard, to lead its fight against 'false populism'. In *The People v. Democracy*, Mounk repeatedly echoes Blair. 'Defenders of liberal democracy', he writes, 'will simply fan the flames of populism if they disregard fears about ineffective border controls or dismiss the degree of public anger about current levels of immigration.' Just as Blair argues that there is no point in 'appearing obsessive on issues like gender identity' – presumably to avoid further wounding the 'white working class', the new holy cow of chastened metropolitans – Mounk indicts a spoiler 'left' for being damagingly obsessed with identity politics, cultural appropriation and shutting down free speech.

An 'anti-totalitarian liberalism', Moyn warned in 2006, as liberal democrats waged war on Islamofascism, 'has become the favoured approach of many political elites in Western democracies.' It seems an ineradicable intellectual reflex as Mounk resurrects in his book the popular oppositions of the Cold War and the war on terror: liberal democracy versus authoritarianism, freedom versus its enemies. Framing these Manicheanisms not as geopolitical challenges but as the West's domestic problem, he suggests a quasi-solution: an 'inclusive nationalism', which Obama and Macron have already articulated in their speeches. We need to focus on what 'unites rather than what divides us', whereas the left is guilty of a 'radical rejection of the nation and all its trappings'. But how does one rebuild a 'collective form of belonging' in the racially and ethnically heterogeneous West? Mounk concedes that 'we cannot recreate the threat of communism or fascism.' Nevertheless, 'we can remember that civics education is an essential bulwark against authoritarian temptations.' Students, taught 'disdain for our inherited political institutions' and encouraged to be suspicious of the Enlightenment, ought to be trained to be 'proud defenders of liberal democracy'. 'Rhetoric matters,' he insists. Hillary Clinton, for instance, 'needed to convince voters that she was passionate about changing the status quo'.

These and other miscellaneous insights, hailed by the *New Yorker* as 'trenchant' and the *Guardian* as 'extraordinary', are useful largely in confirming the persistence of the *ancien régime* in Atlanticist editorial boards, political science departments, think tanks and television studios. Blair, lucratively counselling despots and plutocrats abroad while avoiding citizen's arrest at home, may no longer seem a viable leader of global change. But his project of renewing the centre appeals viscerally to the anti-totalitarian liberals for whom the collapse of the Berlin Wall confirmed once and for all that there is no alternative, and who were consequently blindsided by Trump. These exponents of deregulation, privatisation and pre-emptive wars are the ones most susceptible to Mounk's fables, in which America was moving towards the 'realisation of its high-minded conception' before the way was blocked by an ogre. 'Then came Donald Trump,' Mounk declares, a president who 'openly disdains basic constitutional norms'.

The qualifier 'openly' suggests that the most objectionable thing about Trump may be his discarding of the veil that conceals the scramble for power and wealth among the traditional ruling classes. Mounk does not consider the possibility that the official mendacity concerning illegal wars and assaults on civil liberties may have made some people sceptical about the norms of liberal democracy. He is tactfully silent about the way some leading liberal democrats – Blair, but also Clinton, Lagarde, Schröder, Hollande, Rajoy, Renzi, Cameron and Osborne – are continually caught in the revolving door between business and politics. He doesn't mention either that it was Obama who, as Moyn has put it, 'enhanced the powers of a presidency . . . which is now in the hands of a charlatan', or that in his effort to appease the Republican far right, Obama deported immigrants at a higher rate than Trump has so far. Macron, another of Mounk's cherished liberal democrats, has, while pushing extensive privatisation, unfurled a policy on migrants and refugees so harsh that the Front National celebrates it as a 'political victory'.

There is nothing new about such pragmatic patriots aiming to beat right-wing populists at their own game. Contrary to Mounk's morality tale about liberal democracy, mainstream parties of the centre-left as well as the right have deployed the methods of what Stuart Hall called 'authoritarian populism' ever since the oil shocks and the recessions of the 1970s and 1980s. Hall coined this term in the late 1970s to describe 'the rise of the radical right under Thatcherite auspices' from the ruins of 'the social-democratic consensus'. With capitalism afflicted by an unresolvable structural crisis, fresh populist consent had to be mobilised – often through moral panics about immigrants – for the imposition of harsh neo-liberal policies. Thirty years later, even New Labour resorted, towards the end of its tenure, to authoritarian populism. As an article in the *Utopian*, an American Web magazine, pointed out in 2010, Blair had 'dragged Britain into the Iraq War' on the basis of blatant falsehoods and then 'adopted the most restrictive anti-terror legislation in Europe'. There was an 'authoritarian streak' in both Blair and Brown, who 'ratcheted up coercion' because of 'their failure to make real economic improvements'. Economic growth, 'heavily centred on the financial industry', was 'achieved at the price of ever-new presents to bankers and the super-rich'. As a result, 'Britain's abject underclass has actually continued to grow' and many in the 'disaffected white working class' had either drifted away from electoral politics or embraced such radical rightists as the BNP. 'Labour's populism', the article concluded, 'is a desperate attempt to win back this milieu.'

The author of this combative and prescient analysis – of how the centre had failed to hold and rough beasts started to slouch towards Bethlehem long before Trump made his run for the presidency – was Yascha Mounk. In 2010 he deplored Blair's 'desperate pandering' to the far right and the 'super-rich', and seemed to sympathise with those on the British left who 'think that it's high time to give New Labour the mercy shot'. Working now to rejuvenate Blairism, Mounk re-enacts the original sin of his employer and many other superannuated centrists: the replacement of principle with triangulation.

Samuel Moyn's career is one of reversed affinities: from youthful enchantment with the muzak of the Third Way to rediscovery of *L'Internationale*, from eager collaboration with power to tough-minded scrutiny of it. In 1999, during NATO's bombing of Yugoslavia, Moyn went to Washington, DC, to work as an intern on Clinton's National Security Council. Today, he is a prominent presence in the intellectual culture of the American left, which, denied representation by a mainstream media busy execrating Trump and boosting Never Trumpists, has suddenly flowered in new periodicals (*Jacobin*, *Viewpoint*, *Current Affairs*, the *Los Angeles Review of Books*) and in the revitalised pages of the *Baffler*, the *Boston Review*, *Dissent*, *n+1*, the *New Republic* and the *Nation*. Sceptical of zealous anti-Trumpism, Moyn has chosen – in a time of 'transition from an era of liberal ascendancy to one of liberal crisis' – to excavate the 'egalitarian ideals and practices' that a triumphant neo-liberal capitalism drove underground.

Back in 1999, Moyn was bewitched by the idea of America administering justice to the world's afflicted and benighted. He wasn't alone. The 1990s were prodigal with illusions generated by the collapse of communist regimes, the retreat of social democracy in Europe and the abandonment of socialist ideals in post-colonial Asia and Africa. The ethical vacuum had been filled by human rights, which were entrusted, as Moyn wrote, with 'the grand political mission of providing a global framework for the achievement of freedom, identity, and prosperity'. It was in 1999 that Blair announced in Chicago, 'We are all internationals now, whether we like it or not.' Western values and interests had miraculously merged, and it was imperative to 'establish and spread the values of liberty, the rule of law, human rights and an open society' – by force, if necessary. The first Gulf War, ostensibly fought for the human rights of Kuwaitis, had already helped crystallise a creed in which national sovereignty was no longer inviolate. Human rights, commanding universal approval, came in useful in trashing the principle that had given small countries some protection against superpowers during the Cold War.

Intellectual, moral and legal backing for the New World Order came from a variety of sources. Human Rights Watch supported Washington's disastrous military foray into Somalia in 1992. Jürgen Habermas persuaded himself, briefly, that the US could create a global cosmopolis in the spirit of Kant. John Rawls, transplanting his theory of justice into the realm of international relations, declared in 1999 that societies that violate human rights rightly provoke economic sanctions and military intervention. Liberal peoples, who are naturally indifferent to imperial glory, can justly wage wars of self-defence on 'outlaw' states. The synergy between the aims of the US State Department, human rights advocates and military humanists grew more intense after 9/11. Philip Bobbitt, counsellor to several American administrations, and muse to Blair and Cameron, asserted in *The Shield of Achilles: War, Peace and the Course of History* that 'no state's sovereignty is unimpeachable if it studiedly spurns parliamentary institutions and human rights protections.' In *A Problem from Hell: America and the Age of Genocide*, also published in 2002, Samantha Power outlined the correct response to the world's evildoers: American unilateralism untrammelled by international institutions. Trumpeting Bush's pre-emptive assault on Iraq, Michael Ignatieff recommended in 2003 a new American empire whose 'grace notes are free markets, human rights and democracy, enforced by the most awesome military power the world has ever known'.

The United States, Power asserted as Obama's nominee for US ambassador to the United Nations in 2013, 'is the greatest country on Earth', and 'the leader in human dignity'. She promised that she would 'never apologise for America' and also pledged to 'stand up for Israel and work tirelessly to defend it'. The following year she tweeted a picture of her and Henry Kissinger enjoying a baseball game at Yankee Stadium, and told the *New Yorker* that 'as time wears on, I find myself gravitating more and more to the G.S.D. [Get-Shit-Done] people.' This also seems true of Ignatieff, Power's former colleague at Harvard's Carr Centre for Human Rights Policy, who outlined 'permissible' forms of torture in the *New York Times*; his recommendations (which included 'keeping prisoners in hoods') appeared inconveniently just as the first pictures of a hooded Iraqi prisoner emerged from Abu Ghraib. Ambitious academics such as these have been especially keen to propose American resolve and virtue as a solution to various problems from hell. But it is also the case that human rights, lacking secure legal and philosophical foundation, are prone to appropriation by imperialist regimes as well as by their victims. Once framed as indivisible from the spread of free markets and other good things necessary to the design of Pax Americana, the promotion of human rights could be represented as part of the Pentagon's mission and as a natural corollary of the Washington consensus – just how shit gets done. It also helped that human rights at the end of history offered a seductive 'anti-politics', which, Tony Judt lamented in *Ill Fares the Land*, 'misled a generation of young activists into believing that, conventional avenues of change being hopelessly clogged, they should forsake political organisation for single-issue, non-governmental groups unsullied by compromise'.

Moyn was one of these activists, but has since fruitfully disavowed his youthful romanticism. His work can be read as one long clarification of the way in which the responsibility to protect became indistinguishable from the right to bomb or blockade perceived enemies (Yugoslavia, Afghanistan, Iraq, Syria), the right to nurture 'friends' (Saudi Arabia, Egypt, Israel), and the right to be passive in the face of 'market fundamentalists' as they boosted 'the global rich higher over their inferiors than they had ever been'. In *The Last Utopia*, he attacked the self-congratulatory notion, vended by Ignatieff and others, that awareness of the Holocaust's horrors after the war helped consecrate human rights in a 'revolution of moral concern'. For one thing, Moyn writes, 'there was no widespread Holocaust consciousness in the postwar era.' And few people directly cited the 1948 UN Declaration of Human Rights in the 1950s and 1960s. The discourse of human rights became popular only in the 1970s. Intellectuals, particularly in France, used it to replace their faith in socialism and Third Worldism, and to consecrate an anti-totalitarian liberalism. Politicians such as Jimmy Carter weaponised it in a new ideological and moral offensive against the Soviet Union.

Moyn's new book shows how human rights, as well as enabling American militarism, acquiesced, as a 'powerless companion of market fundamentalism', to the global 'explosion of inequality'. It was in the 1970s that the human rights movement came together, with its particular infrastructure, bureaucracy and fundraising programmes, into what David Kennedy in *The Rights of Spring*, his acidulous memoir of human rights activism in Uruguay in 1984, called the 'smooth and knowing routines of professional advocacy'. Kennedy, recalling time spent in the offices of Human Rights Watch in the Empire State Building, describes the way in which, throughout the 1980s and 1990s, Western human rights groups honed their strategy of 'naming and shaming from a great height'. This model of human rights became hegemonic, though it was far from being universal. In South Africa, for instance, left-wing anti-apartheid activists from the 1970s onwards used the language of rights to demand a broader democratic transformation as well as to defend the victims of state brutality.

What differentiated the Western model from many Asian, African and Latin American networks of women's groups and indigenous peoples, or alternative development and environmental organisations, was its indifference to 'economic and social rights': what Moyn defines as 'entitlements to work, education, social assistance, health, housing, food and water'. Focusing on the violations of individuals' rights by states, human rights groups valuably documented the crimes of the Contras in Nicaragua, the army and death squads in El Salvador, and state terrorists in Guatemala. But they were largely indifferent to the abuse of power by non-state actors: the kleptocratic oligarchies that emerged in Asia, Africa and Latin America throughout the 1990s and 2000s. Nor did they have much to say about the terrible effects of the structural-adjustment programmes implemented by the IMF and the World Bank in the 1980s and 1990s. Human rights politics and law, Moyn argues, may have sensitised us 'to the misery of visible indigence alongside the horrific repression of authoritarian and totalitarian states – but not to the crisis of national welfare, the stagnation of the middle classes and the endurance of global hierarchy'.

Moyn's stern appraisal may not appear new to long-standing critics of Western moral rhetoric in the Global South. Anti-colonial leaders and thinkers knew that the global economy forged by Western imperialism had to be radically restructured in order even partially to fulfil the central promise of national self-determination, let alone socialism. Western liberals were widely perceived as 'false friends', as Conor Cruise O'Brien reported from Africa in the 1960s, and liberalism itself as an 'ingratiating moral mask which a toughly acquisitive society wears before the world it robs'. Distrust of the Western discourse of human rights was likewise constant and deep. The Indonesian thinker Soedjatmoko challenged its presumption of universal morality, pointing to the global inequalities perpetuated by the champions of human rights. Arundhati Roy spoke in 2004 of an 'alarming shift of paradigm': 'Even among the well-intentioned, the expansive, magnificent concept of justice is gradually being substituted with the reduced, far more fragile discourse of "human rights"' – a minimalist request, basically, not to be killed, tortured or unjustly imprisoned. As a result, she argued, 'resistance movements in poor countries . . . view human rights NGOs as modern-day missionaries,' complicit in the West's attempt to impose an 'unjust political and economic structure on the world'.

Some African-American activists saw from the outset that human rights, in their hegemonic American formulation, were not meant to facilitate a 'politics of fair distribution'. Even as the Universal Declaration of Human Rights was being drafted in the late 1940s, W.E.B. Du Bois observed that, as Moyn puts it, 'human rights inevitably became bound up with the power of the powerful.' As Carol Anderson showed in *Eyes off the Prize* and *Bourgeois Radicals*, the National Association for the Advancement of Coloured People (NAACP), helped by Du Bois, appealed in 1947 to the newly established UN to acknowledge African Americans as victims of human rights violations, where violations were defined in this case not only as slavery, Jim Crow and denial of voting rights, but as discrimination in criminal justice, education, housing, employment and access to healthcare. Du Bois and other civil rights leaders echoed the argument of many anti-colonial activists that legal and political rights were impossible to achieve without economic security, and that a mere ban on discrimination would not address centuries of devastation. They ran into vigorous opposition not only from white supremacists among southern Democrats and conservative Republicans, but also from their supposed allies: the Truman administration and Eleanor Roosevelt, for example, who told Du Bois that he was embarrassing the United States before the Soviet Union. Some worried that the demand reeked of socialism. None of them wanted the UN to have any influence in the domestic arrangements of the US. Eventually, the NAACP caved in to the defenders of white supremacy, and sidelined Du Bois. Abandoning its own broad definition of human rights, the NAACP settled for the narrow aim of legal equality. Not surprisingly, deep inequalities in education, healthcare and housing persist to this day: the logic of a human rights movement born and nurtured under the American imperium.

In *The Last Utopia*, Moyn mentioned Du Bois's attempt to internationalise the plight of African Americans and to define institutionalised racism as a human rights violation, but he did not acknowledge the significance of Du Bois's failure to achieve these things, or indeed the many valiant and doomed attempts in the Global South to transcend racialised political and economic hierarchies. Moyn now acknowledges that his previous analysis was incomplete. In *Not Enough*, he more effectively provincialises an ineffectual and obsolete Western model of human rights. As he puts it, 'local and global economic justice requires redesigning markets or at least redistributing from the rich to the rest, something that naming and shaming are never likely to achieve.' Since the human rights movement 'cannot reinvent itself with new ideals and tools', he argues, it should 'stick to what it does best: informing our concepts of citizenship and stigmatising evil, without purporting to stand for the whole of "global justice"'.

Moyn's book is part of a renewed attention to the political and intellectual ferment of decolonialisation, and joins a sharpening interrogation of the liberal order and of the institutions of global governance created by, and arguably for, Pax Americana. In *A World of Struggle: How Power, Law and Expertise Shape Global Political Economy*, David Kennedy blames humanitarian interventionists and international lawyers, among other globalists, for bringing forth a world that is 'terribly unjust, subject to crisis, environmentally unwise, everywhere politically and economically captured by the few'. Martha Nussbaum recently denounced the United Nations 'system' as 'grotesquely flawed and corrupt, totally lacking in democratic accountability, and therefore devoid of any procedural legitimacy when it comes to imposing law on people'. The loss of legitimacy seems more devastating in the case of the West-led human rights movement, for which severe self-reckoning and downsizing seem unavoidable today. Having turned, as David Rieff put it recently in *Foreign Policy*, into a 'secular church of liberal globalism', the human rights movement has become a casualty of the worldwide backlash against liberal globalists. A principled minority long suspicious of Western NGOs has been joined by opportunistic chieftains of majoritarian movements. Erdoğan has jailed the chair of Amnesty International Turkey. Amnesty International India had temporarily to close its offices in Bangalore in 2016 after it was assaulted by Hindu nationalists accusing the charity of 'sedition'. Netanyahu has deported the director of Israel and Palestine Human Rights Watch. In Hungary, Orbán seems determined to expel George Soros's Open Society. As Trump frankly admires autocrats and refuses to pay even vice's meagre tribute to virtue, the human rights movement is facing, as Rieff writes, 'the greatest test it has confronted since its emergence in the 1970s'.

The days when young people transposed their political idealism into the vernacular of liberal internationalism seem to be behind us. Young men and women are more likely today to join domestic political upsurges against neo-liberalism than to fall for a human rights anti-politics miraculously placed beyond political economy. They can hardly avoid noticing the great chasm that now exists between the continuing official commitment to human rights and their brazen infraction in relations everywhere between the rich and the poor, the powerful and the weak. Moyn's own book, probably his last word on the last utopia, looks at democratic vistas beyond the horizons of human rights and a liberalism parasitic on varying evils – communism, Islamofascism, Trumpism – for its self-definition. His timing seems right. 'It is as if the main problem for liberal democracy were its enemies,' Moyn wrote in 2006, introducing a collection of Pierre Rosanvallon's writings, 'as if there were no need to ponder the historical variations and untried possibilities of democracy.' Twelve years later, Trump has inadvertently forced open political and economic possibilities across the ideological spectrum; the Thatcherite assumption that there is no alternative is no longer tenable. Moyn, in *Not Enough*, senses that the crisis of neo-liberalism presents an intellectual and political opportunity. He recovers forgotten moments from the long post-colonial effort to extend to economics and geopolitics the principle of equality that liberals regard as legitimate only in the political realm. He lingers on the proposals made by poor countries in the 1970s for an international economic order that could protect them from the depredations of rich countries and multinational corporations. He describes at length the thinking behind European commitments to national welfare states in the post-war era. This is not nostalgia, of the kind Tony Judt felt for the social democracy of his youth. Nor is it Third Worldism, as a touchy reviewer of Moyn's book in the *New York Times* charged. Rather, Moyn wants to reinstate socialism – which was, after all, the 'central language of justice' globally before it was supplanted by human rights – as an ethical ideal and political objective.

This may seem like a quixotic project. The scale of the left's defeat in recent decades – whether measured in a moribund labour movement, privatised essential services and utilities, economic inequality of Gilded Age proportions, racial resegregation or the backlash against feminism – cannot be concealed. But then the ideals of equality and redistribution never seemed more attractive than when liberalism, having promised universal prosperity and greater democracy, plunged into the slaughterhouse of the First World War, followed by the deepest economic slump in history. The fortunes of socialism have yet again risen as the structural malaise of capitalism is diagnosed more and more clearly by its victims, and conscious collective intervention rather than the invisible hand appears to be the only viable solution to an unfolding environmental catastrophe.

'Socialism', the *Wall Street Journal* nervously reported late last year, 'has moved from being a taboo because of its associations with the Cold War to something that has found rising appeal.' Predictably, the ideological police of the liberal order is working hard to reinstitute the old taboo. Denunciations of a supposedly almighty and fanatical left flow as frequently from the *New York Times*, *Washington Post*, *Boston Globe*, *New York* and *Atlantic* as from Breitbart, and detestation of 'social justice warriors' unites figures as seemingly disparate as Mark Lilla, Steven Pinker, Elon Musk, Niall Ferguson and Jordan Peterson. Bernie Sanders's insurgent campaign confirmed, however, that socialist ideals exist, beyond the experience of communist tyranny, as what John Stuart Mill called 'one of the most valuable elements of human improvement'. Unquestionably, that curious global conjuncture in which neoliberal capitalism and technological leaps forward guaranteed endless progress, and a tiny elite passed off its interests as universal norms, has passed. The appeal of equality as a legal claim and democratic norm has grown and grown – and is paradoxically attested to by anti-establishment uprisings derided as 'populist' threats to liberal democracy. It is unlikely to be defused by attempts to rebuild the liberal order on Macron-style yuppie populism, inclusive nationalism, pragmatic patriotism or any other expedient of an intellectually insolvent (though materially resourceful) centrism. Moyn's book offers no alternative programme of institutional reconstruction or mass mobilisation. But its critical – and self-critical – energy is consistently bracing, and is surely a condition of restoring the pursuit of equality and justice as an indispensable modern tradition.

2018

13

The Final Religion

On Alexander Herzen and Liberalism

The Soviet-subsidised mobile bookshops that enlivened my provincial childhood in the India of the late 1970s and early 1980s always had, in among the English translations of Marx, Lenin and various socialist-realist novels, an edition of Alexander Herzen's novel *Who Is to Blame?*. The title was irresistible and its theme of stupor and futility in the provinces seemed both contemporary and urgent. The 'tryst with destiny' promised by Nehru in 1947 seemed further away than ever in an India that was failing to catch up with the West and become a modern, prosperous and equitable country.

I knew very little about Herzen's background when I first read his work. I had no idea, for instance, that he belonged to the politically engaged generation of Turgenev, Belinsky and Bakunin that emerged in the 1830s and 1840s just as Russia's failure to catch up with a dynamic Europe became painfully apparent. Nor did I know that this scion of a gentry family, banished by the tsarist regime for his activism, had spent much of his life in Europe, among such agitators and polemicists as Marx and Mazzini, and had suffered the usual fate of the political expatriate: betrayal by comrades, the scorn of a younger and more radical generation, isolation and heartbreak. The introductory material in the Soviet edition raised him to the pantheon of Russian radicals; he had displayed, Lenin wrote, 'a selfless devotion' to the cause of revolution. It was puzzling, therefore, when I encountered Herzen a few years later in Isaiah Berlin's essays as a proto anti-communist: someone who had foreseen the dangers of utopian thinking, which can exact human sacrifices in the present for the sake of an imaginary future. In Berlin's writings, which introduced Herzen to Anglo-American readers, he came to resemble a pragmatic Cold War liberal rather than a revolutionary socialist.

Berlin's portrait (or self-portrait) has stood largely unaltered for more than half a century. Herzen's work has not had consistent backing inside or outside academia, on the left or on the right, and *The Discovery of Chance: The Life and Thought of Alexander Herzen*, Aileen Kelly's new biography is unlikely to provoke a revival, or the sort of steady engagement that has continuously enlarged the reputations of Marx and Nietzsche. Unlike Marx, his acrimonious rival, Herzen did not provide a systematic diagnosis of the suffering caused by globalising capitalists, let alone a quasi-scientific plan of salvation. 'Logical truth', he warned, 'is not the same as the truth of history.' Infatuated with Hegel, like many of his young peers in Russia, Herzen later became bluntly dismissive of rational schemata in politics. History, he wrote, contains 'a great deal that is fortuitous, stupid, unsuccessful and confused. Reason, fully developed thought, comes last.' He anticipated Nietzsche in his suspicion that modern Western idealism was a substitute religion with very weak foundations, but was too preoccupied by his political and personal life to write extended critiques. His main works are *My Past and Thoughts*, a mix of memoir, essays and letters, and *From the Other Shore*, a confession of his loss of faith in European ideologies of progress. They offer a complex idea of just who this disillusioned child of nineteenth-century Europe's failed revolutions and revolts thought was to blame. Herzen's perspective, weirdly, still feels unfamiliar after two centuries of Russian, Asian and African journeys to the West: that of the awestruck outsider who eventually comes to question his cravings for redemption through Western modernity.

Born in 1812, the year of Napoleon's disastrous invasion of Russia, Herzen was determined to liberate his country from serfdom and enlist it in the march of progress launched by the scientific and political revolutions in Western Europe. Kelly lingers thoughtfully at the landmarks Herzen passed on his intellectual and political passage through the first half of the nineteenth century: Schiller, Hegel, Saint-Simon, Fourier, George Sand, Feuerbach, Louis Blanc and, crucially, Proudhon. The young Herzen, awed and fascinated by European ideas and achievements, tended to blame the tsars for his country's pitiable backwardness. The Slavophiles and gradualists who preached caution instead of radical transformation were also responsible. But, after he left Russia for good in 1847, living mainly in London as well as in Geneva and Paris, he identified a more insidious culprit: the self-aggrandising bourgeois, who with his gunboats and equivocating ideology of liberalism was coercing and seducing the rest of the world into joining his pursuit of economic self-interest.

Herzen wrote to Turgenev in 1862 that all those who had grown up lamenting Russian barbarousness and idealising the West had 'to recognise with all calm and meekness that the bourgeoisie is the final form of Western European civilisation'. The pursuit of liberty and equality was imperative, and emancipation from the feudal, monarchical and religious world 'essential', but the petite bourgeoisie had shown 'themselves emancipated, not only from monarchs and slavery but from all social obligations, except that of contributing to the hire of government who guarded their security'. The civilisation he admired had turned out to be enjoyed by a 'minority' and 'made possible only by the existence of a majority of proletarians'.

Europhile Russians like himself, he wrote, had been naively trying to replicate in their own country a 'one-sided development, a monstrosity', a heartless way of life, 'which has developed consistently on the basis of a landless proletariat and the unconditional right of the owner over his property'.

'As the knight was the prototype of the feudal world,' he wrote, 'so the merchant has become the prototype of the new world.' Consequently, 'life has been reduced to a perpetual struggle for money . . . everything that is European in the modern sense has two characteristics that clearly stem from this trading mentality: on the one hand, hypocrisy and underhandedness; on the other, exhibitionism and window-dressing.'

His disillusion made Herzen retreat into romantic visions of his ancestral land. He claimed to prefer the Russian 'commune', since it had remained impervious to the lure of private wealth creation. The Russian peasant, untainted by bourgeois self-seeking, seemed to him better equipped to achieve the golden mean between social cohesion and individual freedom. Herzen also came to have a fresh regard for posh Russians like himself: even if they were idle and aimless their 'malady' did not have 'the deeply penetrating, deeply rooted, subtle, nervous, intelligent, fatal depravity from which the educated classes of Western Europe are decaying, suffering and dying'.

Herzen's broadsides ring as true as anything in *The Eighteenth Brumaire*, especially his mockery of British Parliamentary debates for their empty ritual and mere 'appearance of *doing something*'. But his political judgements are not easily separated from his aesthetic and moral ones. Reading John Stuart Mill made him think about the 'conglomerated mediocrity' that surrounded him in Britain: 'the narrowing of men's minds and energies', 'the constant increasing superficiality of life', and 'general human interests' being 'reduced to the interests of the counting-house and bourgeois prosperity'. Rather than Tocqueville's laboratory of democracy, America seemed to him a 'cold, calculating country'. As for the French, they are 'the most abstract and the most religious people in the world', who 'turn everything into an idol, and woe to him who will not bow before the idol of the day'.

The time he spent in France before and after the failed revolution of 1848 introduced him to a resourceful bourgeoisie that had long ago subverted the ideals of 1789. But unlike Marx, who devised ever more ambitious schemes for supplanting the bourgeoisie with the working class, Herzen came to conclude that the 'prevailing tone' could not be altered, though political agitators would continue to disrupt it. 'Emancipation', he concluded, 'has finally proved to be as insolvent as redemption.' The revolutions 'have lit new desires in the hearts of men, but they have not provided ways of satisfying them.' And so 'the yearning peoples appear, wearied with struggle and way-worn: "I have no liberty, I have no equality, I have no fraternity."' But the bourgeois 'goes on muttering incoherent phrases about progress and liberty'. Herzen recognised, as Marx never could, that demagogues would routinely emerge to offer the exhausted and cheated masses the opiate of nationalism: 'The classification of men by nationalities', he wrote in the 1840s, 'becomes more and more the wretched ideal of the world which has buried the revolution.' He would have immediately recognised the line that leads from the undermining of socialism and social democracy to white nationalism.

Kelly's *tour d'horizon* of nineteenth-century thought describes how Herzen came to attack the notions of human agency implicit in teleological programmes of progress. It is good to see the visionary Proudhon, the pioneering theorist of anarchist socialism, rescued from his dismal intellectual fate as just another of Marx's many targets. And Kelly writes in interesting detail about the influence on Herzen of Francis Bacon and Charles Darwin. But the passion – and torment – that drove Herzen flashes only intermittently in her book. Kelly quotes Tolstoy saying that 'Herzen awaits his readers in the future. Far above the heads of the present crowd, he transmits his thoughts to those who will be able to comprehend them.' Her own attempt to present Herzen as an intellectual hero of our time doesn't always break free of the oppositions of Cold War liberalism: his work, she writes, 'can now be seen as a uniquely prescient indictment of the political messianism that attained its evil maturity only in the next century and marked that century for all time with its imprint'.

Herzen, however, pioneered much more fruitful modes of intellectual and moral analysis than anti-totalitarianism. He argued with Westernising liberals in Russia who saw a strong state as the engine of secular modernity. Herzen feared that these partisans of 'reasonable freedom and moderate progress', steeped in political economy and legal theory, would 'reconcile us with all that we despise and hate' by strengthening the centralised bureaucracy. By destroying their traditional forms of organisation, they would expose peasants to violence and famine. At best, he wrote, 'in a century and a half their improvements will lead to the state from which Prussia is seeking to escape.' This is an eerily precise indictment of the self-proclaimed liberals of post-colonial Asia and Africa whose efforts at top-down modernisation ended up reinforcing the repressive colonial state.

He also rose above an intellectual parochialism to which the Eurocentric Marx was not immune: 'Europe', Herzen pointed out, 'resolves everything in the world by analogy with itself.' He rejected its notionally universal path of progress, arguing that countries needed to find their own way, which was always contingent on local circumstances. 'Why', he asked, 'should a nation that has developed in its own way, under completely different conditions from those of the West European states, with different elements in its life, live through the European past, and that, too, when it knows perfectly well what that past leads to?'

His criticism of the narcissism of Western ideologues and Westernised policy makers anticipated that of many disenchanted close observers of the West from the keenly imitative East. Dostoevsky was among the unlikely figures who borrowed from the incendiary anti-Westernism of *From the Other Shore*. Many travellers from the East, such as the Indian poet Rabindranath Tagore, the Chinese thinker Liang Qichao and the Islamist agitator Sayyid Qutb, would have found little to disagree with. Deploring the bourgeoisie's homogeneous culture of acquisition and consumption, Herzen came to respect human diversity not just as an abstract value but as a prerequisite for intellectual and aesthetic originality. Claude Lévi-Strauss, who defended premodern societies against accusations of backwardness, would have endorsed his view that 'each phase of historical development has had its end in itself, and hence its own reward and satisfaction.' Most important, those appalled by the undermining of political life by global commercial, ideological and financial nexuses would recognise Herzen's insight into the early stages of this process. The 'consequences of the supremacy of trade and industry', he wrote, are that the shopkeeper is at the 'helm of the world', forcing the government to become his 'shop assistant'. It is undoubtedly clearer today, with the revolving doors between business, politics and the media spinning ever faster, that 'everything – the publication of newspapers, the elections, the legislative chambers – all have become moneychangers' shops and markets.'

Herzen objected most vigorously not to communism but to the *'final religion'*, as he termed the faith of liberals – the defiant italics are his – whose 'church is not of the other world but of this' and whose 'theology is political theory', the 'last word of civilisation founded on the absolute despotism of property'. He saw through the self-image of a philosophy and politics that claimed to oppose the state on behalf of individual freedom, but imposed its principles with the help of the state's tools of violence and coercion, as in the imperialist wars waged on behalf of free trade. 'Liberalism', he wrote, 'has learned ever more artfully to unite a constant protest against the government with a constant submission to it.' It's not hard to guess what he would have made of neo-liberals, who constantly protest against government while depending on it to extend the market's coldly evaluative assessments to all aspects of human life (and to lock up the unproductive and the superfluous in ever-expanding prisons).

Herzen's great achievement was to identify the power that cannily assigns inescapable destinies to individuals in line with their capacity to be competitive and profitable while at the same time paying lip service to universal progress, equality and liberty. 'Petite bourgeoisie', he lamented, 'is the idea to which Europe is striving, and rising from every point on the ground.' He failed to anticipate that all human societies would one day be organised around the bleak project of competitive self-aggrandisement, and that all those trying to catch up with the modern West would reproduce the dialectic of bourgeois 'miserliness' and plebeian 'envy' and the grim synthesis of ethnic–racial nationalism. But our demagogic present nevertheless vindicates the warnings of this Russian latecomer to modernity that 'race hatreds and bloody collisions' would result from the general 'ignorance' about the *'final religion'* and its zealots.

2017

14

Bumbling Chumocrats

On British Elites and Brexit

Describing Britain's calamitous exit from its Indian empire in 1947, the novelist Paul Scott wrote that in India the British 'came to the end of themselves as they were' – that is, to the end of their exalted idea about themselves. Scott was among those shocked by how hastily and ruthlessly the British, who had ruled India for more than a century, condemned it to fragmentation and anarchy; how Louis Mountbatten, accurately described by the right-wing historian Andrew Roberts as a 'mendacious, intellectually limited hustler', came to preside, as the last British viceroy of India, over the destiny of some 400 million people.

Britain's rupture with the European Union is proving to be another act of moral dereliction by the country's rulers. The Brexiteers, pursuing a fantasy of imperial-era strength and self-sufficiency, have repeatedly revealed their hubris, mulishness and ineptitude over the past two years. Though originally a 'Remainer', Prime Minister Theresa May has matched their arrogant obduracy, imposing a patently unworkable timetable of two years on Brexit and laying down red lines that undermined negotiations with Brussels and doomed her deal to resoundingly bipartisan rejection in Parliament.

Such a pattern of egotistic and destructive behaviour by the British elite flabbergasts many people today. But it was already manifest seven decades ago during Britain's rash exit from India.

Mountbatten, derided as 'Master of Disaster' in British naval circles, was a representative member of a small group of upper- and middle-class British men from which the imperial masters of Asia and Africa were recruited. Abysmally equipped for their immense responsibilities, they were nevertheless allowed by Britain's brute imperial power to blunder through the world – a 'world of whose richness and subtlety', as E. M. Forster wrote in 'Notes on the English Character', they could 'have no conception'.

Forster blamed Britain's political fiascos on its privately educated men, callow beneficiaries of the country's elitist public-school system. These eternal schoolboys whose 'weight is out of all proportion' to their numbers are certainly overrepresented among Tories. They have today plunged Britain into its worst crisis, exposing its incestuous and self-serving ruling class like never before.

From David Cameron, who recklessly gambled his country's future on a referendum in order to isolate some whingers in his Conservative Party, to the opportunistic Boris Johnson, who jumped on the Brexit bandwagon to secure the prime ministerial chair once warmed by his role model Winston Churchill, and the top-hatted, theatrically retro Jacob Rees-Mogg, whose fund management company has set up an office within the European Union even as he vehemently scorns it, the British political class has offered to the world an astounding spectacle of mendacious, intellectually limited hustlers.

Even a columnist for the *Economist*, an organ of the British elite, now professes dismay over 'Oxford chums' who coast through life on 'bluff rather than expertise'. 'Britain', the magazine belatedly lamented last month, 'is governed by a self-involved clique that rewards group membership above competence and self-confidence above expertise.' In Brexit, the British 'chumocracy', the column declared, 'has finally met its Waterloo'.

It is actually more accurate, for those invoking British history, to say that partition – the British Empire's ruinous exit strategy – has come home. In a grotesque irony, borders imposed in 1921 on Ireland, England's first colony, have proved to be the biggest stumbling block for the English Brexiteers chasing imperial virility. Moreover, Britain itself faces the prospect of partition if Brexit, a primarily English demand, is achieved and Scottish nationalists renew their call for independence.

It is a measure of English Brexiteers' political acumen that they were initially oblivious to the volatile Irish question and contemptuous of the Scottish one. Ireland was cynically partitioned to ensure that Protestant settlers outnumber native Catholics in one part of the country. The division provoked decades of violence and consumed thousands of lives. It was partly healed in 1998, when a peace agreement removed the need for security checks along the British-imposed partition line.

The reimposition of a customs and immigration regime along Britain's only land border with the European Union was always likely to be resisted with violence. But Brexiteers, awakening late to this ominous possibility, have tried to deny it. A leaked recording revealed Mr Johnson scorning concerns about the border as 'pure millennium-bug stuff'.

Politicians and journalists in Ireland are understandably aghast over the aggressive ignorance of English Brexiteers. Businesspeople everywhere are outraged by their cavalier disregard for the economic consequences of new borders. But none of this would surprise anyone who knows of the unconscionable breeziness with which the British ruling class first drew lines through Asia and Africa and then doomed the people living across them to endless suffering.

The malign incompetence of the Brexiteers was precisely prefigured during Britain's exit from India in 1947, most strikingly in the lack of orderly preparation for it. The British government had announced that India would have independence by June 1948. In the first week of June 1947, however, Mountbatten suddenly proclaimed that the transfer of power would happen on 15 August 1947 – a 'ludicrously early date', as he himself blurted out. In July, a British lawyer named Cyril Radcliffe was entrusted with the task of drawing new boundaries of a country he had never previously visited.

Given only around five weeks to invent the political geography of an India flanked by an eastern and a western wing called Pakistan, Radcliffe failed to visit any villages, communities, rivers or forests along the border he planned to demarcate. Dividing agricultural hinterlands from port cities, and abruptly reducing Hindus, Muslims and Sikhs on either side of the new border to religious minorities, Radcliffe delivered a plan for partition that effectively sentenced millions to death or desolation while bringing him the highest-ranked knighthood.

Up to one million people died, countless women were abducted and raped, and the world's largest refugee population was created during the population transfers across Radcliffe's border – an extensive carnage that exceeds all apocalyptic scenarios of Brexit.

In retrospect, Mountbatten had even less reason than Mrs May to speed up the exit clock – and create insoluble and eternal problems. Just a few months after the botched partition, for instance, India and Pakistan were fighting a war over the disputed territory of Kashmir. None of the concerned parties were pushing for a hasty British exit. As the historian Alex von Tunzelmann points out, 'the rush was Mountbatten's, and his alone.'

Mountbatten was actually less pig-headed than Winston Churchill, whose invocation stiffens the spines of many Brexiteers today. Churchill, a fanatical imperialist, worked harder than any British politician to thwart Indian independence and, as prime minister from 1940 to 1945, did much to compromise it. Seized by a racist fantasy about superior Anglo-Americans, he refused to help Indians cope with famine in 1943 on the grounds that they 'breed like rabbits'.

Needless to say, such ravings issued from an ignorance about India as intractable as that of the Brexiteers about Ireland.

Churchill's own Secretary of State for India claimed that his boss knew 'as much of the Indian problem as George III did of the American colonies'. Churchill displayed in his long career a similarly imperial insouciance toward Ireland, sending countless young Irishmen to their deaths in a catastrophic military fiasco at Gallipoli, Turkey, during the First World War and unleashing brutal paramilitaries against Irish nationalists in 1920.

The many crimes of the empire's bumptious adventurers were enabled by Britain's great geopolitical power and then obscured by its cultural prestige. This is why images cherished by the British elite of itself as valiant, wise and benevolent could survive, until recently, much damning historical evidence about these masters of disaster from Cyprus to Malaysia, Palestine to South Africa. In recent years, such privately educated and smooth-tongued men as Niall Ferguson and Tony Blair could even present the British as saviours of suffering and benighted humanity, urging American neoconservatives to take up the white man's burden globally.

Humiliations in neo-imperialist ventures abroad, followed by the rolling calamity of Brexit at home, have cruelly exposed the bluff of what Hannah Arendt called the 'quixotic fools of imperialism'. As partition comes home, threatening bloodshed in Ireland and secession in Scotland, and an unimaginable chaos of no-deal Brexit looms, ordinary British people stand to suffer from the untreatable exit wounds once inflicted by Britain's bumbling chumocrats on millions of Asians and Africans. More ugly historical ironies may yet waylay Britain on its treacherous road to Brexit. But it is safe to say that a long-cosseted British ruling class has finally come to the end of itself as it was.

15

The *Economist* and Liberalism

'Liberalism made the modern world,' the *Economist* lamented in 2018, on its 175th anniversary, but 'the modern world is turning against it'. Europe and America are 'in the throes of a popular rebellion against liberal elites' while authoritarian China is about to become the world's largest economy. For a weekly magazine 'created 175 years ago to campaign for liberalism', and to serve as a how-to manual for liberal elites, this can only be 'profoundly worrying'. Certainly, the magazine's view that liberalism is in crisis has become received wisdom across a broad spectrum. No less a liberal than Barack Obama included Patrick Deneen's *Why Liberalism Failed* in his annual list of recommended books, while Vladimir Putin gleefully pronounces liberalism 'obsolete'. The right accuses liberalism of promoting selfish individualism and crass materialism at the expense of social cohesion and cultural identity. Centrists charge that liberals' obsession with political correctness and minority rights drove white voters to Donald Trump. For the newly resurgent left, the rise of demagoguery looks like payback for the small-government doctrines of technocratic neo-liberalism – tax cuts, privatisation, financial deregulation, anti-labour legislation, cuts in social security – which have shaped policy in Europe and America since the 1980s.

Liberalism is best known for its famous enemies, and its recent critics enlist in a diverse and vital tradition. In 1843, the year the *Economist* was founded, Karl Marx wrote, 'The glorious robes of liberalism have fallen away, and the most repulsive despotism stands revealed for all the world to see.' Nietzsche dismissed John Stuart Mill, the author of the canonical liberal text 'On Liberty' (1859), as a 'numbskull'. In colonialised Asia and Africa, critics – such as R. C. Dutt in India, and Sun Yat-sen in China – pointed out liberalism's complicity in Western imperialism. Muhammad Abduh, the grand mufti of Egypt, wrote, 'Your liberalness we see plainly is only for yourselves.' (Mill, indeed, had justified colonialism on the ground that it would lead to the improvement of 'barbarians'.) This prejudice was more widely confirmed after the end of the First World War when US President Woodrow Wilson, while claiming that his 'liberalism is the only thing that can save civilization from chaos', upheld global white supremacy, presiding over a peace treaty that divided the spoils of the war among European imperialists.

Liberalism by then had provoked many other negative assessments in Germany, Italy and Japan – three countries urgently trying to match Anglo-America's economic and geopolitical power. Many British and American thinkers, ranging from Reinhold Niebuhr to John Gray, went on to point out that liberalism has a troubled relationship with democracy and human rights, and too complacent a belief in reason and progress. Yet these numerous criticisms of liberalism, made in different economic and political settings, make it no easier to figure out what precisely is being criticised.

Much confusion about this philosophy of individual liberty arises because liberalism connotes both a freedom of regulation from the state in economic life – the dominant definition of recent decades that makes liberalism resemble libertarianism – and also a demand, notably implemented by New Deal progressives in the US and post-Second World War governments in Britain, for the state to ensure a minimal degree of social and economic justice.

The canonical figures of liberalism themselves moved between these contradictory commitments. John Stuart Mill, the *ur*-liberal for many, also called himself a socialist, outlining an aim that the *Economist* would surely find illiberal: 'common ownership in the raw materials of the globe'. John Dewey claimed the label 'liberal' for himself as soon as it acquired common currency in the United States in the early twentieth century. The Great Depression forced him to conclude in 1935 that 'the socialized economy is the means of free individual development.' Isaiah Berlin upheld non-interference from the state as the superior of what he called in his celebrated 1958 lecture 'Two Concepts of Liberty'. Eleven years later, Berlin came to see such 'negative liberty' as enabling 'politically and socially destructive policies' that armed 'the able and ruthless against the less gifted and less fortunate'.

It is tempting to leap across three centuries and locate the unwavering core of liberalism in John Locke's treatises on individual reason, tolerance and property rights. Isaiah Berlin, after all, insisted that liberalism was an 'English invention'. But Locke, a devout Christian and stockholder in a slaveholding company, was not regarded as a philosopher of liberalism until the mid-twentieth century. Indeed, recent scholars have argued that liberalism acquired inner coherence and intellectual ancestry only as the default 'other' of the twentieth century's 'totalitarian' ideologies of the left and right. By the time the Cold War began, it could even seem synonymous with 'democracy', 'capitalism' and 'the West' in general, its moral prestige underwriting such coinages as 'liberal capitalism' and 'liberal democracy'. Thus Lionel Trilling could claim in 1950 that liberalism in America is 'not only the dominant but even the sole intellectual tradition'. Re-emerging as a 'fighting faith' after the terrorist attacks of 9/11, liberalism seemed more than ever to define the West against such illiberal enemies as Islamofascism and authoritarian China.

The *Economist* proudly enlists itself in this combative Anglo-American tradition of liberalism that was elaborated, if not invented, during the Cold War. In its own account last year of making the modern world, 'liberalism spread in the nineteenth and twentieth centuries against the backdrop first of British naval hegemony and, later, the economic and military rise of the United States.' In *Liberalism at Large*, his history of the magazine, Alexander Zevin takes the *Economist* at its word, examining the sayings and deeds of a formidable Anglo-American elite that has vigorously claimed, from the mid-nineteenth century to the present, to be liberals and to be universally advancing liberalism. Such a method not only clears much conceptual muddle about liberalism. It opens up a view on actually existing and widely practised liberalisms over 175 years: how, conjoined with British and then American military, cultural and economic power, they truly made the modern world, if not quite how many self-declared liberals have seen it.

Zevin, a professor at City University of New York, has found an exceptionally illuminating and oddly under-covered subject in the *Economist* – a magazine like no other in its circulation and influence. Marx saw the London-based weekly in the 1850s as expressing the concerns of the British 'aristocracy of finance'. By 1895, Woodrow Wilson had declared it to be 'a sort of financial providence for businessmen on both sides of the Atlantic' (the Anglophile Wilson wooed his clearly forbearing wife with quotations from Walter Bagehot, the most famous of the *Economist*'s editors). Although the magazine was long proud of an exclusive readership, it now has nearly a million subscribers in North America (more than it does in Britain) and 300,000 in the rest of the world. Since the early 1990s, it has served, alongside the *Financial Times*, as the suavely British-accented voice of globalisation (scoring over the too stridently partisan and American *Wall Street Journal*).

According to its own statistics, its readers are the richest and the most prodigal consumers among readers of periodicals anywhere; more than 20 per cent once claimed ownership of 'a cellar of vintage wines'. The *Economist* itself invokes, like Aston Martin, Burberry and other global British brands, the glamour of elitism. 'It's lonely at the top,' one of its ads reads, 'but at least there's something to read.' Articles, almost all unsigned, were until recently edited from an office in St James's, London, a redoubt of posh Englishness with its private clubs, cigar merchants, hatters and tailors. The present editor is the first woman to ever to hold the position. The staff, predominantly white, are recruited overwhelmingly from the universities of Oxford and Cambridge – a disproportionate number of the most important editors have come from just one Oxford college, Magdalen. 'Lack of diversity is a benefit,' Gideon Rachman, a former editor who is now a columnist at the *Financial Times*, told Zevin, explaining that it produces an assertive and coherent point of view.

Indeed, the contributors are not shy of adding prescription (how to fix India's power problems and so on) to their reporting and analysis. The pieces are mostly short. Yet the coverage is comprehensive – a single issue might cover, say, the insurgency in south Thailand, public transport in Jakarta, commodities prices and recent advances in artificial intelligence – and this air of crisp editorial omniscience ensures that it is as likely to be found on an aspirant think-tanker's iPad in New Delhi as in Bill Gates's private jet.

Zevin, having evidently mastered the magazine's archives, commands a deep knowledge of its inner workings, and its historical connection to political and economic power. He shows how its editors and contributors pioneered the revolving door between media, politics, business and finance – alumni have gone on to such jobs as deputy governor of the Bank of England, prime minister of Britain, and president of Italy – and how such men have defined, at crucial moments in history, liberalism's ever-changing relationship with capitalism, imperialism, democracy and war.

A capsule version of Zevin's thesis can be found in the career of James Wilson, a struggling Scottish hat manufacturer who founded the *Economist* and became its first editor. Wilson hoped for the weekly to oppose agricultural tariffs, and to develop and disseminate the doctrine of laissez faire – 'nothing but pure principles', as Wilson put it. Successful in a cause favoured by business interests – the Corn Laws, as the tariffs were called, were repealed in 1847 – Wilson went on to proselytise more energetically through his magazine for free trade and the then rising discipline of economics. He became a Member of Parliament and held several positions with the British government. He also founded a pan-Asian bank, now known as the Standard Chartered bank, which expanded fast on the back of the opium trade with China. In 1859, Wilson became 'Chancellor of the Indian Exchequer'. He died in India the following year, trying to reconfigure the country's financial system.

Wilson briskly clarified during his short career as a journalist-cum-crusader what he meant by 'pure principles'. He opposed a ban on trading with slaveholding countries since it 'would hurt British consumers and punish slaves'. Responding to the Irish famine, largely caused by free trade, Wilson called for a homeopathic remedy: more free trade. With Irish intransigence becoming a nuisance, Wilson called upon the British to respond with 'powerful, resolute, but just repression'. Wilson was equally stern with those suffering from rising inequality at home. In his view, the government was wrong to oblige rail companies to provide a better service for working-class passengers, who were forced to travel in exposed freight cars: 'Where the most profit is made, the public is best served . . . limit the profit, and you limit the exertion of ingenuity in a thousand ways.' On these grounds, a factory bill limiting working hours for women to twelve was deemed equally pernicious. As for public education, common people should be 'left to provide education as they provide food for themselves'.

The *Economist*'s earliest position, from which it has rarely departed, was that 'if the pursuit of self-interest, left equally free for all, does not lead to the general welfare, no system of government can accomplish it.' It turned out, however, that government was always necessary to vanquish the enemies of liberalism. As Zevin describes it, wars against Russia and China, and conflicts in India, in the 1850s 'rocked British liberalism at home and recast it abroad'. Free-traders had consistently claimed that what they did was the best hedge against war. But, expanding forcefully across Asia, and often imposing free trade at gunpoint, the British provoked conflict, and for the *Economist* wherever Britain's 'imperial interests were at stake, war could become an absolute necessity, to be embraced'.

The betrayal of principle alienated, among others, the businessman and statesman Richard Cobden, who had helped Wilson found the *Economist*, and shared his early view of free trade as a guarantee of world peace. India for Cobden was a 'country we do not know how to govern', and Indians were justified in rebelling against an inept despotism. For Wilson's *Economist*, however, Indians, as much as the Irish, exemplified the 'native character . . . half child, half savage, actuated by sudden and unreasoning impulses'. Also, 'commerce with India would be at an end were English power withdrawn.' Cobden found such arguments 'sophistical'. He may have felt vindicated by the *Economist*'s view of slavery and the American Civil War under its second editor, Walter Bagehot, who broadened the appeal of his father-in-law's invention, largely by applying much intellectual gloss to sophistry. Bagehot was personally sympathetic to the Confederacy, convinced that it could not be defeated by the northern states, whose 'other contests have been against naked Indians and degenerate and undisciplined Mexicans.' He also believed that abolition was best achieved by a southern victory. More importantly, trade would be freer with the southern states.

~

Detailing the *Economist*'s startlingly numerous misjudgements of the nineteenth and twentieth centuries, Zevin's method is not that of a twenty-first-century virtue signaller. He seems genuinely intrigued by how the liberal vision of individual freedom and international harmony was 'transmuted', as Niebuhr once put it, 'into the sorry realities of an international capitalism which recognized neither moral scruples nor political restraints in expanding its power over the world'. Zevin's sociology of liberalism's elites shows how it became the self-legitimating ideology of a rich, powerful and networked ruling class; how liberalism's original meaning was transformed by its later exponents under the pressures of capitalist expansion abroad and rising mass disaffection at home.

Private ambition played no less a role in liberalism's steady mutation. Bagehot stood for Parliament four times as a member of Britain's Liberal Party. Born in a family of bankers, he saw himself and his magazine as offering counsel to a new generation of buccaneering British financiers. His tenure coincided with 'the age of capital', when British finance capital transformed the world economy, expanding food cultivation in North America and Eastern Europe, cotton manufacturing in India, mineral extraction in Australia and rail networks everywhere. According to Zevin, 'it fell to Bagehot's *Economist* to map this new world, tracing the theoretical insights of political economy to the people and places men of business were sending their money.'

Zevin most fruitfully describes how liberals coped with the growing demand for democracy. Bagehot, who had read and admired John Stuart Mill as a young man, finally agreed with him only about the need to civilise the natives of Ireland and India. He found absurd Mill's idea of broadly extending the suffrage to women. Nor could he support Mill's proposal for enfranchising the labouring classes in Britain, reminding his readers that 'a political combination of the lower classes, as such and for their own objects, is an evil of the first magnitude.' Not surprisingly, the *Economist* commended Mussolini (a devoted reader) for sorting out an Italian economy destabilised by labour unrest.

By the early twentieth century, the magazine was groping towards the awareness that classical liberalism had to be moderated in an advanced industrial society and that ruling classes had to embrace progressive taxation and basic social-welfare systems in order to defuse rising discontent. The magazine presents this volte-face as evidence of its pragmatic liberalism. Zevin reveals it as a grudging response to rising democratic pressures from below. Moreover, there were clear limits to the *Economist*'s freshly compassionate liberalism. As late as the 1910s, one editor, Francis Hirst, was still denouncing 'the shrieking, struggling, fighting viragoes' who had demanded the right to vote despite having no capacity for reason. (His comparison of suffragettes to Russian and Turkish marauders – pillaging 'solemn vows, ties of love and affection, honour, romance' helped drive his own wife away.)

The *Economist* was finally forced to compromise on its pure principles as more people acquired the right to vote and market mechanisms failed, empowering autocrats and accelerating international conflicts. In a book celebrating the magazine's centenary in 1943, its then editor acknowledged that larger electorates saw 'inequality and insecurity' as a serious problem. Disagreement with the socialists was 'not on their objective, but only on the methods they proposed for attaining it'. Such a stance mirrored a widespread acceptance on both sides of the Atlantic that governments should do more to protect their citizens from an inherently volatile economic system. Since the 1960s, however, the *Economist* has steadily reinstated its foundational ideals.

In the process, it missed an opportunity to reconfigure its imperial-era liberalism for the post-colonial age, to make its old dogma, enforced through military force, about the free circulation of capital and goods compatible with the new reality of sovereign nation states with underdeveloped economies. As

Zevin relates, the *Economist* saw decolonisation and the emergence of new nation states across Asia and Africa – arguably the most important event of the twentieth century – through the Cold War's binary opposition of the 'free' and 'unfree' world. Yet it failed to engage, in the way that even a Cold War liberal like Raymond Aron did, with the challenges and dilemmas before a vast majority of the world's population – was it prudent, for instance, for a newly sovereign nation of largely poor and illiterate people to embrace free trade right away, before building state and industrial capacity? The magazine's editors increasingly looked to the developed West rather than the developing East for ideas and inspiration, and, more insularly, to economics departments and think tanks, where the pure-market principles of Milton Friedman and Friedrich Hayek were increasingly dominant, rather than to such liberal theorists of justice as John Rawls, Ronald Dworkin and Amartya Sen.

In the 1980s, its cheerleading for Margaret Thatcher and Ronald Reagan's embrace of neo-liberalism led to a dramatic rise in its American circulation (Reagan personally thanked the then editor for his support over dinner at the White House). Dean Acheson famously remarked that 'Great Britain has lost an empire but not yet found a role.' No such status anxiety inhibited the *Economist* as it crossed the Atlantic to make new friends and influence more people with its argument that the post-war settlement in Britain and America impeded growth. After some initial resentment of the new global hegemon, commonplace among British elites after the end of the Second World War, the *Economist* adjusted itself to Pax Americana; it came to revere the US as, in the words of one editor, 'a giant elder brother, a source of reassurance, trust and stability for weaker members of the family, and nervousness and uncertainty for any budding bullies'.

This meant stalwart support for American interventions abroad, starting with Vietnam, where, as historian and former staff writer Hugh Brogan put it, the magazine's coverage

was 'pure CIA propaganda'. Euphemising the war's horrors –
incidents like the My Lai massacre were seen as 'minor variations on the general theme of the fallibility of men at war' –
the magazine was complaining by 1972, following the satura-
tion bombing of North Vietnam, that Henry Kissinger was too
soft on the North Vietnamese. A policy of fealty to the giant
elder brother also made some campaigners for liberalism a bit
too prone to skullduggery. Zevin details some colourful stories
about the magazine's over-zealous Cold Warriors, such as
Robert Moss, who diligently prepared international opinion
for the military coup in Chile that brought down its democrati-
cally elected leader Salvador Allende in 1973. According to Moss,
'Chile's generals reached the conclusion that democracy does
not have the right to commit suicide.' (The generals expressed
their gratitude by buying and distributing 9,750 copies of the
Economist). Zevin relates that when news of Allende's death
reached him in London, Moss danced down the corridors of
the *Economist*'s office chanting, 'My enemy is dead!' He went
on to edit a magazine owned by Nicaragua's US-backed dictator
Anastasio Somoza.

After the collapse of communist regimes in 1989, the *Economist*
embraced a fervently activist role in Russia and Eastern Europe,
armed with the mantras of privatisation and deregulation.
Jeffrey Sachs, one of the 'Harvard Boys' expounding 'transition economics' in Eastern Europe and Russia, coined the term
'shock therapy' in a special article in 1990 for the *Economist*
with the suitably Leninist title 'What Is to Be Done?'. The brutal
socio-economic re-engineering recommended by Harvard and
Oxbridge boys climaxed in Russia's financial implosion in 1998,
setting the stage for a popular autocrat, who duly emerged in
2000 promising to restore order. In November 1997, a few
months before this Putin-enabling disaster, the *Economist* was
still hailing the 'dynamism, guile and vision' of Anatoly Chubais,
by then the most despised public figure in Russia for organising

the fire sale of his country's assets to oligarchs. A 2009 study in the *Lancet* claimed that 'shock therapy' led to the premature death of millions of Russians, mostly men of employment age. The magazine was unrepentant in its response: 'Russia's tragedy', it insisted, 'was that reform came too slowly, not too fast.'

As editors dined at the White House and 10 Downing Street, or went to work for the British government and the Bank of England, the *Economist* enjoyed in recent decades ever-greater opportunities to speak its truths to power. Now, with the political class on both sides of the Atlantic breaking bad, it is lonelier at the top for the *Economist* than at any other time in its existence. A cover story in October 2019 – 'Who Can Trust Trump's America?' – forlornly summed up the devastation wrought by recent political earthquakes on assumptions nurtured during the Cold War and unhealthily fattened after the end of history. In 2006, an *Economist* cover story praised Goldman Sachs for its mastery of risk, hailing 'the development of huge markets in swaps, derivatives and other complex and often opaque instruments'. When the financial crisis erupted, the magazine overcame its primal distrust of government intervention to endorse the taxpayer's bailouts of banks, arguing that 'this is a time to put dogma and politics to one side.' 'The people running the system,' it concluded, 'not the system itself, are to blame.' Accordingly, it continued to defend the system and all that apparently made it unbeatable: lower tariffs, greater privatisation, accelerated public-sector downsizing.

Finally chastened, if not by the financial crisis then by its grisly political upshot, the magazine concedes in last year's manifesto for 'renewing liberalism' that 'liberals have become too comfortable with power,' and are seen as 'self-serving and unable, or unwilling, to solve the problems of ordinary people'. It now hopes to reinvent 'liberalism for the people'. But those tempted to say 'bring it on' would not be encouraged by a manifesto that admiringly quotes Milton Friedman on the need to be 'radical', and, while resurrecting John McCain's fantasy of a 'league of democracies' as an alternative to the United Nations, scoffs at 'younger people' who don't wish to fight for the old 'liberal world order'. A recent cover story warns 'American bosses' against Elizabeth Warren's plans to tackle inequality while resurrecting Friedman-ite verities about how 'creative destruction' and 'the dynamic power of markets' can best help 'middle-class Americans'.

The *Economist* is no doubt sincere about wanting to be more 'woke'. Having rushed in 2002 to the barricades on behalf of Bjorn Lomborg, the global-warming sceptic, it dedicated an entire issue to the climate emergency this autumn. It seeks more female readers, according to a 2016 briefing for advertisers, and is anxious to dispel the impression of the magazine 'as an arrogant, dull handbook for outdated men'. Still, the magazine may find it more difficult than most in the old Anglo-American establishment to check its privilege. Its limitations arise not only from a defiantly un-diverse and parochial intellectual culture, but also from a house style prone to contrarianism. A 2014 review in the *Economist* of a book titled *The Half Has Never Been Told: Slavery and the Making of American Capitalism* accused its author of a lack of 'objectivity', complaining that 'almost all the blacks in his book are victims, almost all the whites villains.' Following an outcry, the magazine retracted the book review. However, a recent headline – 'Jair Bolsonaro Is a Dangerous Populist, with Some Good Ideas' – over an article that endorsed the Brazilian leader's plan to deregulate and privatise confirms that it is hard to tone down what the journalist James Fallows once described as the magazine's 'Oxford Union argumentative style': a stance too 'cocksure of its rightness and superiority'.

This insouciance has been bred by the certainty of having made the modern world. It can only seem incongruous in the rancorously polarised societies of Britain and the United States. The two crazy-haired demagogues ruling the world's oldest 'liberal' democracies confirm that a ruling class that failed to foresee, and that even ideologically enabled, a global financial crisis, serenely presided over intolerable levels of inequality, and despoiled large parts of the Middle East, Central Asia and North Africa with ill-conceived military interventions, has squandered its authority and legitimacy. The assumption, central to much Cold War liberalism, of England as a model liberal society, where liberalism was invented, also lies shattered amid the calamity of Brexit.

For the young, in particular, old frameworks of liberalism seem to be a constraint on the possibilities of politics. It should be remembered, however, that these new critics of liberalism seek not to destroy but to fulfil its promise of individual freedom. They seek to find, just as John Dewey did, suitable modes of politics and economy in a fast-changing world – a liberalism for the people, not just for their networked rulers. In that sense, liberalism is not so much in crisis as are its self-styled campaigners, whom many see, not unreasonably, as complicit in unmaking the modern world.

2019

16

England's Last Roar

'We have got to fight against privilege,' George Orwell exhorted in 1941, 'against the notion that a half-witted public-schoolboy is better for command than an intelligent mechanic.' England, he wrote, is governed by an 'unteachable' ruling class that too frequently escapes into 'stupidity', failing to see 'that an economic system in which land, factories, mines and transport are owned privately and operated solely for profit – *does not work*'.

Only a socialist revolution could unleash the 'native genius of the English people'. Of course, 'the bankers and the larger businessmen, the landowners and dividend-drawers, the officials with their prehensile bottoms, will obstruct for all they are worth'. But, never mind: 'If the rich squeal audibly, so much the better.'

One measure of how little has changed is that Orwell's diagnosis of the country he called a 'rich man's paradise' – and even his specific prescriptions: nationalization of basic industries, abolition of hereditary privilege, educational reform and punitive taxation of offensively unequal incomes – still resonates, almost eight decades later, as the United Kingdom goes to the polls. The long English past of entrenched privilege and extreme inequality is back, if it ever went away. The problems stemming from archaic political and social structures, and an economy geared to further enriching the rich, seem even more intractable.

At the same time, the wartime English patriotism that Orwell tried to alchemize into socialism as highly intelligent Germans tried to kill him, has degenerated into self-destructive nihilism during the Tory onslaught on a German-dominated European Union – ready to countenance even the breakup of the Union.

Fragmentation of the United Kingdom would of course leave the Welsh and the Scottish with a sharper sense of their political and cultural identity. Englishness, on the other hand, seems as foggy as ever. As the hunters of an authentic English national identity, pursued differently by Orwell, Enoch Powell and, most recently, the Brexiteers, lurch towards a political climax, it seems worth asking: what is it all about?

Englishness was always a form of theatre, first scripted and staged in England's colonies. Discovering its traces in Kipling and India, V. S. Naipaul remarked on how 'at the height of their power, the British gave the impression of a people at play, a people playing at being English, playing at being English of a certain class'. Today, in a post-imperial Britain run by half-witted public schoolboys, the English 'character' seems even more, as Naipaul wrote, 'a creation of fantasy'.

Those who saw through the fantasy were usually mortified, such as Orwell. Born in Bengal to an opium agent, with one Caribbean slave-owner as his ancestor, Orwell worked as a colonial policeman in Burma and while doing so discovered imperialism to be an 'evil despotism' and Englishness a humiliating act: a pose of masculine authority and racial superiority necessary to keep volatile natives in their place.

Others, such as Powell, a lower middle-class native of the West Midlands, were seduced precisely by this posture of stiff-upper-lipped preeminence. Powell became a classicist at Cambridge, taught himself fox-hunting, and wrote highly wrought Georgian verse; he exulted, as a brigadier, in the hierarchies of empire in India. Then, like Curzon, Milner, Cromer and other purveyors of an Englishness made in India and Egypt, he came to develop, once back home, a certain rather fierce idea of England and its destiny.

Orwell, on the other hand, was an archetype of the unpatriotic left-winger on his return home – until he found a lodestone of native English genius in the presently cracking 'red wall' of North England. The spirited English response to Hitler's vicious assault deepened his conviction of having discovered a new 'emotional unity' in England – one that a socialist revolution could turn in favour of its trampled-upon peoples. He persuaded himself that 'England, together with the rest of the world, is changing', and a new middle class blending in with the old working class would bring forth 'new blood, new men, new ideas'.

War did indeed awaken a spirit of social egalitarianism, leading to Conservative defeat in 1945. Some of Orwell's proposals were partially implemented by the Atlee government. Still, there was always something too sanguine about the homecoming scenario of a deracinated intellectual.

For, if England was a family, as Orwell claimed, with 'rich relations who have to be kow-towed to, and poor relations who are horribly sat upon', then, as a range of foreign and English observers noted at the time, it was a family marked to an unusual degree by sadomasochistic relationships.

J.G. Ballard, another disaffected child of imperialism, who arrived in England in 1946 after three years in a Japanese internment camp in Shanghai, was not only appalled by his country's 'grotesque social division'. He also marvelled at the impregnable 'system of self-delusions' that enabled a people comparable in their poor education, diet and grim housing to the menial toilers of Shanghai to give their lives to 'an empire that had never been of the least benefit to them'.

'The English class system, which everyone secretly accepted, for reasons I have never understood', Ballard later wrote, was an 'instrument of political control'. Far from collaborating on revolution, the straitened middle class feared and despised the working classes, especially organized labour, and was obsessed with enforcing codes of behaviour that were 'calculated to create a sense of overpowering deference'.

As for the upper class, Edmund Wilson noted in 1945 how its members manifested the 'appalling' traits he had found in novels such as *Vanity Fair* and *The Way of All Flesh*: 'passion for social privilege' and 'dependence on inherited advantage'. Janet Frame, discussing the seemingly unbreakable social hierarchy of England's natives with other indigent New Zealanders and Australians in London in the 1950s, concluded, 'They're in the Middle Ages.'

'Change, I felt, was what England desperately needed,' Ballard, reminiscing about the 1940s, wrote two years before his death in 2009, 'and I still feel it.' Yet England's political and social system had long been premised on regulating change when it favored the middle class and neutralizing it when demanded by the working classes, while all the time safeguarding the unteachably stupid upper class. Walter Bagehot, the *Economist* editor with an acute phobia for England's poor and disenfranchised, put it frankly in 1867: the unwritten 'English constitution in its palpable form is this – the mass of the people yield obedience to the select few'; they 'defer to what we may call the theatrical show of society'.

Discussing the role of the monarchy in this theatre, Bagehot was equally blunt: 'We must not let in daylight upon magic.' In other words, the masses of England were to be ruled by almost the same combination of pomp, bluff and repression that the natives of India were. The fossilized politics enjoyed greater legitimacy at home because the English had lived through much of the modern era as its winners, innovating industrially and expanding commercially well before other countries; the mystique of British power commanded deference, while perpetuating such archaisms as a single parliament representing four nationalities. Though as exploited and defrauded as Indians, the English people, Orwell wrote, 'manifestly tolerated' their selfish, incompetent and often 'silly' ruling class; the 'post-war development of cheap luxuries' in particular 'averted revolution'.

~

The *Economist* reassured itself in 1977: 'Britain's very stability, the beguiling flummery attending its institutions, hold most of its citizens in a trance of acceptance.' But the trance had begun to break after 1945, when instead of enlarging the realm on which the sun never set, the English began to retreat, and, simultaneous with the loss of colonial territories, the colonized started to arrive in a war-ravaged England.

Enoch Powell, among others, had cherished a starry-eyed notion of the empire as a large multiracial family (with white males on top). But the unstated proviso for an imperialist pater-familias was always that the dark-skinned family members stay put in their respective countries and not seek to live, work and marry white people in England. The new arrivals in England, prompted by the post-war need for NHS nurses, bus drivers and other workers, quickly exposed this separate-but-equal chicanery of the 'Commonwealth'.

Writing in 1953 to his wife, Naipaul summed up the hostile environment the British Empire's previously invisible citizens confronted in England. Considered only 'for jobs as porters in kitchens, and with the road gangs', the Oxford-educated Trinidadian had been reduced, he claimed, to a 'poor wog, literally starving, and very cold' with 'no fire in my room for two days and only tea & toast in my stomach'. 'These people want to break my spirit,' Naipaul wrote. 'They want me to forget my dignity as a human being.'

The fact that most people from the colonies inhabited even lower depths of poverty, humiliation and despair had little effect on public opinion and policy. Racialized immigration acts were passed throughout the 1960s; the poor wogs were also repeatedly put in their place by the police, the media and politicians. A Tory candidate in Powell's own stomping ground, the West Midlands, won his election in 1964 with the campaign slogan 'If you want a nigger for a neighbour, vote Labour.'

Still, those accustomed to lording it over dark-skinned natives in the outposts of Empire could not be appeased. If, as Naipaul wrote, 'to be English in India was to be larger than life', then to be English in multiracial England after 1945 was to know a devastating loss of manliness. Decolonization had been outrageous enough for Powell, who had hoped as late as 1951 for Churchill to reconquer his great love, India. The appearance on English streets of dangerous savages against whom Englishness had been defined on the imperial frontier was just too much.

The racial hierarchy in which he had found his being was in danger of being overturned. As he put it (quoting an unnamed, 'quite ordinary' person), 'In this country in fifteen or twenty years' time the black man will have the whip hand over the white man.' There was also something intolerable about the fact that imperialism had become, if not a source of shame and embarrassment, then a subject for comedy and satire among a younger generation – summed up by the album cover of *Sgt. Pepper's*. Upstart darkies and cheekily androgynous Liverpudlians together turned the 1960s into a hellish time for Brigadier Powell.

'What sort of people do we think we are?' he thundered in 1967. One self-pitying answer was: a 'nation of ditherers'. The following year, Powell mutated into a ventriloquist for the silent majority – members of the white working class who worried about immigration, were denounced for their honesty by 'piccaninnies' as racist, and were ignored by 'academics, journalists, politicians and parties'. In a classic sleight-of-hand of intellectual demagoguery, the former professor of Ancient Greek claimed to be only articulating 'plain truths and commonsense' that 'decent, ordinary' people, bullied by a politically correct establishment, did not dare express.

The usual temptation to hold foreigners and immigrants responsible for decline and stagnation was strong in England as post-war economic growth tapered off. In Kamala Markandaya's outstanding, recently republished, novel *The Nowhere Man* (1972), which is set in the weeks around Powell's 'Rivers of

Blood' speech in April 1968, a white Londoner reduced to living with his wife's mother is greatly relieved to discover that blacks are to blame for his luckless existence. 'A great light bursts upon' him as he receives Powell's newly respectable wisdom: 'They came in hordes, occupied all the houses, filled the hospital beds, and their offspring took all the places in schools.'

Writing in 1969, Paul Foot pointed out that 'new scapegoats must be found for the homelessness, the bad hospital conditions, and the overcrowded schools'. Tom Nairn cautioned, however, against the then common tendency to dismiss Powell as a posh race-baiter or a mustachioed blast from the imperial past. Nairn pointed out that Powell, turning his back on an irretrievably lost empire, had set out to construct a post-imperial English nationalism with a mass base. The problem with English identity always was that it consisted of little more than a theatrical performance of brute power abroad by men of the imperial ruling class. It had lacked any broad content at home (notwithstanding Orwell's infusions of socialism and his belated patriotism). More ambitiously and successfully than Orwell, Powell was now forging a native English genius at home by defining it, initially at least, against emasculating wogs.

Writing in 1970, Nairn predicted a long-term future for Powellism, which 'actively stirs up conflict instead of conspiring to stifle or ignore it' and, in an existential crisis, 'can pull the whole of the official structure of British politics in his direction'. In retrospect, Powell himself charted the high English road to Powellism, as he went on to invest his zeal for stark antagonism in Ulster Unionism, neo-liberalism (he actually confabulated with the Mont Pelerin Society) and, finally, Europhobia: 'Belonging to the Common Market', he wrote in 1975, 'spells living death, the abandonment of all prospect of national rebirth, the end of any possibility of resurgence.'

A very different destiny for post-1945 England, which did not involve quacks vending pills for imperial-era virility, was always likely. The possibilities lay in its multi-racial experience – something genuinely new in England since Orwell's time. Some of the early arrivals in England were deeply damaged by it, such as Naipaul, who escaped from deprivation into the company of those gratified by his scorn for fellow wogs. But many others came to attest to the potential of much more fluid post-imperial identities. 'I am an Englishman, born and bred almost,' a character called Karim Amir declares in Hanif Kureishi's *The Buddha of Suburbia* (1990).

Yet it was, significantly, Powellism that steadily built up to its present political apotheosis in Brexit – through the Thatcher–Blair years of deregulation and privatization and beyond. It fattened on a hardening political consensus against immigration, a tabloidized culture of journalism, and demented Tory EU-baiting, all assisted by the propaganda empire of an Australian media tycoon almost as committed to a politics and culture of xenophobia as his father, a stalwart of White Australia policy.

Until such time as it could hunker down in Westminster, the Brigadier's hyperbolic Englishness renovated its original home in the realm of kitsch. In Julian Barnes' *England, England*, a marketing company desperate to make money out of a country in rapid decay decides to build a theme park of Englishness on the Isle of Wight. A tycoon modelled on Murdoch and Maxwell persuades the Royal Family to move to a more up-to-date copy of Buckingham Palace as real England slides into pre-industrial squalor.

England, England, published a year after the Princess of Wales died and the Millennium Dome began construction, now seems a timely meditation on the fate of English identity. Englishness had descended deeper into parody throughout the 80s and 90s. A Sloane Ranger had let in too much daylight, even paparazzi flashbulbs, upon the magic of the monarchy, while the devolutionary demands of Scotland and Wales uncovered the many fault lines in the notion of Britishness. Many a cultural and intellectual entrepreneur emerged during these decades, ranging from St George flag manufacturers to Churchill fanboys, hectically retailing Englishness and elaborating Powellism in high- as well as low-brow modes.

Roger Scruton, the High Tory philosopher and author of *England: An Elegy*, took up Powell's lament about the despoliation of England, giving it a neo-pastoralist orientation. Scruton, who shared Powell's ancestry in northern England's lower middle class, reinvented himself as a fox-hunting country squire, as prone to defend public schools from his own Labour-voting father's 'resentment' as to sneer at the people who 'litter the country with their illegitimate, uncared-for and state-subsidised offspring'. As Tory–New Labour free-marketeering eviscerated traditional communities and social bonds, Scruton chose to deplore the loss of 'the stiff upper lip' that 'went with imperial pride'.

Scruton in this mode embodied two of the 'quintessences' of Englishness identified by Barnes in *England, England*: 'snobbery' and 'whingeing'. Nevertheless, the vendors of Englishness had judged their market well in the age of Reagan and Thatcher. A televised version of *Brideshead Revisited*, a novel breathless in its adoration of the well-born and contempt for everyone else, became the biggest British cultural export since the Beatles to the US (where the series was fittingly presented, in the midst of a Republican-led backlash to the civil rights movement, by William F. Buckley, a right-wing publicist with a loftily mid-Atlantic accent). Bedazzled by Castle Howard, Ralph Lauren repackaged country-house *poshlost* for Americans, and even sold it back to the already Barboured English.

The Raj, lavishly filmed in the 1980s, reappeared in the English imagination as an aesthetic spectacle, provoking awe rather than embarrassment. Many Americans succumbed to this imperial chic as well; and made it more lucrative. Emerging just in time to cash in on empire-mania, Banana Republic's range of khaki colonial wear offered an opportunity to vicariously quell, in jodhpurs and pith helmets, the mutinous natives of Sind and Punjab. In this sense, those British chancers who later crossed the Atlantic to exhort Americans to reestablish empire, and offer their expertise in governing Basra and Helmand, were only following the money.

Arguments for carnage in Mesopotamia definitely sounded more persuasive when made with the Oxbridge cocksureness of a Christopher Hitchens, the Orwell du jour. Indeed, Englishness as a mode of glamorously aloof and omnisciently clever elitism became one of England's chief exports. Orwell had railed against England's 'idle rich', 'living on money that was invested they hardly knew where', and 'whose photographs you can look at in the *Tatler* . . . always supposing that you want to'. Benefitting from a zeitgeist of feeling 'intensely relaxed' about the 'filthy rich', the *Tatler*'s circulation rose and international editions bloomed, ushering the tuxedoed and begowned demi-monde of Jakarta and Manila into the pleasures of Cool Britannia.

Old English nurseries of the imperial ruling class such as Harrow and Wellington opened franchises in Thailand and China, offering to transmit solemn lessons from white supremacy to crazy rich Asians. Two London-based periodicals run by the Oxbridge elite, the *Economist* and *Financial Times*, became the most widely consulted how-to manuals of financial globalisation, sagely instructing wannabes how to think and even spend like the filthy rich.

In J. G. Ballard's last novels, England is reduced to offering up its cultural icons for Disneyfication to the world while preparing itself for authoritarian populism. The reality now seems to have closely approximated Ballard's dystopic fiction all along. For, while Hugh Grant's dimpled grin advertised the charms of the English family, its precious silver was being sold off. In a process witnessed in no other major Western country, almost all the great emblems of national power, prestige and glamour – British Steel, Rolls-Royce, Aston Martin, Bentley, Jaguar, Debenhams, British Home Stores, HMV, Cadbury, Gieves & Hawkes, Hamleys – have either disappeared or gone into foreign hands since the 1980s. A few weeks ago, Thomas Cook, which once sold holidays to Churchill, became insolvent, stranding thousands of customers abroad and forcing the government to mount its biggest civilian rescue operation since Dunkirk.

It is only in such a 'stagnant, involuted atmosphere of a world near the end of its tether' that Powellism could become hegemonic, Tom Nairn predicted in 1970, healing wounded English pride with reactionary balm and appealing 'to the (perfectly justified) national feeling of frustration and anger'. More importantly, 'because this feeling is so inarticulate, and so divorced from the genteel clichés of the Establishment, Powellism could 'suggest convincingly that something is profoundly wrong and that something must be done about it'.

As Boris Johnson never tires of repeating: Get Brexit Done. Nothing like a dose of hard Brexit, he suggests, to toughen the national mind and body for the bracing climb to the sunlit uplands of 'Empire 2.0'. Like Powell, he presents himself as the saviour of England's matchless destiny against the ditherers; like the habitué of Mont Pelerin, he believes that a high dose of deregulation and privatisation will make England great again. More disingenuously than the brigadier, he ridicules the piccaninnies as well as the dangerous aliens in letterboxes and reaches out to the Home Counties' colonels with promises to lock up swarthy criminals and throw away the key. There should be no mistaking the neo-fascistic cults of unity and potency he promotes, and the insidious forms they assume in England's Murdochised media.

In Ballard's last novel *Kingdom Come* (2006), English nationalism turns sadistically against those Powell stigmatized as hostile aliens. However, violent racism, which has exploded in recent years, is not nearly as sinister as the steady hardening of Powellite verities into bien pensant opinion. Centrist Dads as much as unteachable Brexiteers are likely to invoke his much-victimized silent majority of ordinary, decent men, dispossessed by immigrants and then gagged by politically correct academics and journalists. Thus, Simon Jenkins in the *Guardian* last week: Brexit 'was about how far Britons can define and protect the character of where they live'.

With Brexiteers in the ascendant politically as well, the triumph of Powellism is complete. But we may be looking at an instance, to borrow a term from the Bush administration, of 'catastrophic success'. For Powellism remains, in its moment of hegemony, a symptom of rather than a cure for the seemingly insoluble crisis that Orwell diagnosed: the dwindling material basis of an ex-imperialist country that is unable to break, in a globalised world, with its antique assumptions of power and self-sufficiency, and whose fundamentally cynical Bagehotian mode of politics, in which the will of the few was passed off as the will of the many, is broken, unable to innovate and deal with change or defuse the anger of those victimized for so long by social and economic inequity.

'The life of nations,' Powell argued, 'no less than that of men is lived largely in the imagination.' But nations that are too extravagantly imagined eventually pay a steep price for their system of self-delusions. Post-colonial India turns, as its dream of power and glory explodes, upon itself in fury and frustration. England's post-imperial self-reckoning feels harsher, largely because it has been postponed for so long, and the memories of power and glory are so ineradicable. In the meantime, the most important elections of our lifetime approach, and, as Orwell warned, 'A generation of the unteachable is hanging upon us like a necklace of corpses.'

2019

Index